STUDY GUIDE
Mary Gowan
University of Central Florida

EIGHTH EDITION

GARY DESSLER

PRENTICE HALL
UPPER SADDLE RIVER, NJ 07458

Acquisitions editor: Stephanie Johnson
Managing editor: Melissa Steffens
Associate editor: Hersch Doby
Project editor: Richard Bretan
Manufacturer: Integrated Book Technology

© 2000 by Prentice Hall, Inc.
Upper Saddle River, New Jersey 07458

All rights reserved. No part of this publication may be
reproduced, in any form or by any means,
without permission in writing from the publisher.

Printed in the United States of America

10   9   8   7   6   5   4   3   2   1

ISBN 0-13-016406-2

Prentice-Hall International (UK) Limited, London
Prentice-Hall of Australia Pty. Limited, Sydney
Prentice-Hall Canada Inc., Toronto
Prentice-Hall Hispanoamericana, S.A., Mexico
Prentice-Hall of India Private Limited, New Delhi
Prentice-Hall of Japan, Inc., Tokyo
Prentice-Hall (Singapore) Pte Ltd
Editora Prentice-Hall do Brasil, Ltda., Rio de Janeiro

TABLE OF CONTENTS

CHAPTER 1	THE STRATEGIC ROLE OF HRM	1
CHAPTER 2	EQUAL OPPORTUNITY AND THE LAW	8
CHAPTER 3	JOB ANALYSIS	18
CHAPTER 4	PERSONNEL PLANNING AND RECRUITMENT	25
CHAPTER 5	EMPLOYEE TESTING AND SELECTION	33
CHAPTER 6	INTERVIEWING CANDIDATES	41
CHAPTER 7	TRAINING AND DEVELOPING EMPLOYEES	48
CHAPTER 8	MANAGING ORGANIZATIONAL RENEWAL	56
CHAPTER 9	APPRAISING PERFORMANCE	64
CHAPTER 10	MANAGING CAREERS AND FAIR TREATMENT	73
CHAPTER 11	ESTABLISHING PAY PLANS	80
CHAPTER 12	PAY-FOR PERFORMANCE AND FINANCIAL INCENTIVES	88
CHAPTER 13	BENEFITS AND SERVICES	97
CHAPTER 14	LABOR RELATIONS AND COLLECTIVE BARGAINING	105
CHAPTER 15	EMPLOYEE SAFETY	114
CHAPTER 16	MANAGING HR IN AN INTERNATIONAL BUSINESS	121

CHAPTER 1

THE STRATEGIC ROLE OF HUMAN RESOURCE MANAGEMENT

CHAPTER DESCRIPTION

This chapter introduces the concept of human resource management, discusses why this role is important for all managers to understand and properly execute, and describes the role of the human resource department as a strategic business partner.

CHAPTER OBJECTIVES

1. Answer the question: "What is human resource management?"
2. Discuss the components of the changing environment of human resource management.
3. Present examples of the new management practices that are changing human resource management.
4. Describe the nature of strategic planning.
5. Give examples of human resource management's role as a strategic partner in business.

CHAPTER STUDY OUTLINE

I. Human Resource Management at Work
   A. What is human resource management?
      1. Management process: planning, organizing, staffing, leading, and controlling
      2. Human resource management (HRM): practices and policies to carry out personnel aspects of management job
   B. Why is HR management important to all managers?
      1. Reduces likelihood of costly mistakes associated with hiring the wrong people
      2. Reduces risk of lawsuits due to discrimination and other labor violations
   C. Line and staff aspects of HRM
      1. Line versus staff authority
         a. Authority involves right to make decisions and to direct work of others
         b. Line managers direct work of subordinates and are in charge of accomplishing organization's basic goals
         c. Staff managers assist and advise line managers in accomplishing basic goals
      2. Line managers' HRM responsibilities
      3. Human resource department's HRM responsibilities
         a. Line function involves directing personnel in HR manager's own area
         b. Coordinative function consists of functional control of personnel activities
         c. Staff (service) functions assist line managers with hiring, training, etc.
         d. Employee advocacy involves ensuring fair and equitable treatment of employees
      4. HR job duties
         a. Recruiters
         b. Equal employment opportunity (EEO) representatives or affirmative action coordinators
         c. Job analysts
         d. Compensation managers
         e. Training specialists
         f. Labor relations specialists

II. The Changing Environment of Human Resource Management
   A. Changes in organizations
      1. Globalization – tendency of firms to extend sales or manufacturing to new markets abroad
      2. Technological advances – forces firms to become more competitive

3. Deregulation – industry protection once provided by government regulations often no longer exists
4. Trends in nature of work – shift from manufacturing to service jobs
5. Workforce diversity – more women, minority-group members and older workers in workforce
6. Other trends affecting human resource management – new laws being passed

III. Tomorrow's HR Today
   A. New management practices
      1. Traditional, pyramid-shaped organization going out of style
      2. Employees being empowered
      3. Flatter organizations becoming the norm
      4. Work increasingly organized around teams and processes
      5. Bases of power are changing
      6. Managers must build commitment
   B. Changing role of HR management: People and performance
      1. 1900s – HR began handling hiring and firing, payroll, and benefits
      2. 1930s – HR emphasized protecting firm in interaction with unions
      3. 1960s and 1970s – effective personnel practices needed to prevent lawsuits
      4. Currently – HR shifting from being protector to being strategic partner and change agent
   C. HR and employee commitment
   D. HR and performance
      1. HR practices facilitate employee behavior that impacts service
      2. HR responsiveness to company needs can make companies more competitive
      3. Research supports relationship between firm performance and HR practices
   E. HR and corporate strategy

IV. Strategic Planning and HR Management
   A. Nature of strategic planning
      1. Corporate-level – identifies portfolio of businesses
      2. Business-level/competitive strategy – how to build and strengthen long-term competitive position
      3. Functional strategies – identify basic courses of action for each of business's departments
      4. Strategic planning – outlines type of business firm will be
      5. Competitive advantage
         a. Cost leadership
         b. Differentiation
         c. HR
   B. Strategic HRM
   C. HR's role as strategic partner
      1. View 1: HR is operational and not strategic
      2. View 2: HR should fit company's strategy
      3. View 3: HR is equal partner in strategic planning
         a. HR's role in formulating strategy
            (1) Environmental scanning
            (2) Supplying competitive intelligence
            (3) Providing information on internal strengths and weaknesses
         b. HR's role in executing strategy
            (1) HR processes as competitive advantage
            (2) Supporting strategy implementation
         c. HR best practices
            (1) Broad, generally applicable HR principles or philosophies
            (2) Other practices firm or industry specific
         d. Strategic future of HR department
            (1) Belt tightening a trend
            (2) Outsourcing
            (3) Ways to protect HR department

CHAPTER STUDY QUIZZES

Match Terms With Definitions

a. Diversity
b. Globalization
c. Job analysts
d. Competitive intelligence
e. Staffing
f. Staff managers
g. Strategic planning
h. Competitive advantage
i. Labor relations specialists
j. Outsourcing

_____ 1. Deciding what type of people should be hired, recruiting prospective employees and selecting employees.

_____ 2. Managers who are authorized to assist and advise line managers in accomplishing their goals.

_____ 3. HR personnel who collect and examine detailed information about job duties to prepare job descriptions.

_____ 4. HR personnel who advise management on all aspects of union-management relations.

_____ 5. The tendency of firms to extend their sales or manufacturing to new markets abroad.

_____ 6. Any attribute people use to tell themselves that others are different from them (e.g., race, sex).

_____ 7. Type of planning that outlines the type of business the firm will be, given the firm's external opportunities and threats and its internal strengths and weaknesses.

_____ 8. Any factors that allow an organization to differentiate its product or service from those of its competitors to increase market share.

_____ 9. Information about competitors used in the strategic planning process such as details of advanced incentive plans and information about pending legislation.

_____ 10. Having activities such as recruitment and benefits management handled outside the organization.

True/False

1. T F The management function of leading involves setting standards such as quotas.

2. T F HR activities are solely the responsibility of the HR department.

3. T F Staff managers are in charge of accomplishing the organization's basic goals.

4. T F Typical HR positions include compensation managers and job analysts.

5. T F A pronounced shift from service jobs to manufacturing jobs has occurred in North America and Western Europe.

6. T F Between 1992 and 2005, the percentage of people classified as "Asian and other" in the workforce will jump by just over 81%.

7. T F Establishing HR programs that really work is a challenge for employers.

8. T F Employee empowerment involves ensuring that employees will have what they need to serve customers.

9. T F One way HR can help employees adapt to pressures from downsizing is by helping employees learn to prioritize tasks.

10. T F Differences in HR practices of organizations are not associated with differences in financial performance.

11. T F A competitive strategy identifies how to build and strengthen the business's short-term competitive advantage in the marketplace.

12. T F HR management should take first place in the strategic planning process of a firm.

Multiple Choice

1. Human resource management refers to
    a. the five basic functions performed by all managers: planning, organizing, staffing, leading and controlling.
    b. the practices and policies you need to carry out the people or personnel aspects of your management job.
    c. assigning tasks to subordinates, establishing departments, and delegating authority.
    d. setting standards for how and by whom work is to be performed.

2. The implied authority possessed by HR managers results from
    a. the fact that HR managers often have access to top management in personnel areas like testing and affirmative action.
    b. the fact that HR managers assist line managers in the "bread and butter" of the HR manager's job.
    c. the fact that HR managers assist with hiring and firing.
    d. the very nature of the work they perform.

3. The _____ role of human resources involves developing processes for fair treatment of employees by management.
    a. recruitment
    b. employee advocacy
    c. training
    d. compensation administration

4. Which of the following is not a typical HR position you might find in a large company?
    a. industrial nurse
    b. labor relations specialist
    c. compensation manager
    d. engineer

5. Why does HR need to be concerned with globalization?
    a. With more production shifted overseas, HR must develop policies and procedures for managing a global labor force.
    b. Globalization is likely to reduce the need for any kind of HR jobs.
    c. The shift in production overseas changes the functional areas with which HR is concerned.
    d. HR does not need to be concerned with globalization.

6. The knowledge, education, training, skills, and expertise of a firm's workers is referred to as
    a. diversity.
    b. human capital.
    c. human resources.
    d. behaviors.

7. By the year 2005, Hispanics will represent what percentage of the civilian labor force in the U.S.?
   a. 8%
   b. 64%
   c. 11%
   d. 47%

8. In a boundaryless organization, employees
   a. do not have offices but instead carry laptop computers with them to stay connected.
   b. do not identify with separate departments but instead interact with whomever they must to get the job done.
   c. do not have defined job responsibilities.
   d. do not work just in one city or one country.

9. The current focus of human resource management recognizes that
   a. enforcement of EEO laws is the most important task.
   b. the most important role is one of protector.
   c. hiring and firing of employees is the sole responsibility of the human resource department.
   d. it is essential that human resource personnel be change agents and strategic partners.

10. What is one way the United States government found that they could improve performance?
    a. reducing the number of hours employees work each week
    b. providing better work areas for employees
    c. using personnel tests to select high-potential employees
    d. do not replace employees who leave

11. HR is placed in a central role in strategy formulation because
    a. of the recognition that it is often the firm's employees who provide the key to competitiveness.
    b. HR vice presidents have demanded to have input.
    c. of the recognition that HR managers are now professionally trained.
    d. of efforts of the firms to treat all departments equitably.

12. Wal-Mart is a cost leader. This means that Wal-Mart
    a. sets the highest prices in the industry.
    b. is the first to get new products out at a good cost.
    c. is only concerned about cost.
    d. uses techniques such as satellite-based distribution systems to reduce costs.

13. United Airlines and American Airlines both rejected the opportunity to acquire USAir due, in part, to doubts that they could successfully negotiate new labor agreements with USAir's employees. This decision resulted because of _____ which considered HR issues.
    a. competitive intelligence
    b. knowledge management
    c. human capital management
    d. environmental scanning

14. The best guidance relative to managing HR is to
    a. identify best practices of competitors and stick to those.
    b. learn as much as possible about HR practices that work and design an appropriate practice consistent with your company's goals.
    c. recognize that there are no best practices for managing HR.
    d. let managers make their own decisions about what works even though consistent policies will not exist.

15. For HR to be a strategic partner, experts recommend that all but which of the following take place?
    a. become an expert in the way work is organized and executed
    b. become an agent of continuous improvement
    c. become a champion for employees
    d. become focused on only the here and now

Essays

1. Describe what is meant by "human resource management" and discuss who in the organization is responsible for these activities.

2. Identify four trends affecting organizations, giving examples of how these trends specifically impact management of human resources.

3. In what ways are firms changing their management and organization to enhance their competitiveness?

4. Discuss the relationship between human resource management and firm performance.

5. What is meant by the statement that HR must be a strategic partner?

ANSWER KEY

Match Terms with Definitions

1. e (p. 2)
2. f (p. 4)
3. c (p. 5)
4. i (p. 5)
5. b (p. 9)
6. a (p. 12)
7. g (p. 19)
8. h (p. 21)
9. d (p. 24)
10. j (p. 25-26)

True/False

1. F (p. 2)
2. F (p. 2-3)
3. F (p. 4)
4. T (p. 5)
5. F (p. 11)
6. T (p. 12)
7. T (p. 13)
8. T (p. 14)
9. T (p. 18)
10. F (p. 19)
11. F (p. 19)
12. F (p. 22)

Multiple Choice

1. b (p. 2)
2. a (p. 4)
3. b (p. 5)
4. d (p. 5)
5. a (p. 9-10)
6. b (p. 11)
7. c (p. 12)
8. b (p. 14)
9. d (p. 17)
10. c (p. 18)
11. a (p. 19)
12. d (p. 21)
13. d (p. 23)
14. b (p. 25)
15. d (p. 26)

Essay
See the following pages in the textbook for discussion on the essay question topics.

1. Pages 2-5
2. Pages 9-13
3. Pages 13-16
4. Pages 18-19
5. Pages 22-26

CHAPTER 2

EQUAL OPPORTUNITY AND THE LAW

CHAPTER DESCRIPTION

This chapter presents information about the history of equal employment opportunity law, describes current laws, discusses defenses against discrimination allegations, and concludes with a discussion of affirmative action and diversity management issues.

CHAPTER OBJECTIVES

1. Summarize the basic equal employment opportunity laws regarding age, race, sex, national origin, religion and handicap discrimination.
2. Explain the basic defenses against discrimination allegations.
3. Present a summary of what employers can and cannot do with respect to illegal recruitment, selection and promotion, and layoff practices.
4. Explain how to set up an affirmative action program.

CHAPTER STUDY OUTLINE

I. Equal Employment Opportunity 1964-1991
   A. Background
      1. Fifth Amendment (1791)
      2. Thirteenth Amendment (1865)
      3. Fourteenth Amendment (1868)
      4. Civil Rights Act of 1966
   B. Title VII of the 1964 Civil Rights Act (CRA 1964)
      1. What the law says about discrimination
      2. Who does Title VII cover?
      3. The Equal Employment Opportunity Commission (EEOC)
   C. Executive orders
      1. Executive Order 11246
      2. Executive Order 11375
      3. Affirmative Action
      4. Office of Federal Contract Compliance Programs (OFCCP)
   D. Equal Pay Act of 1963
   E. Age Discrimination in Employment Act of 1967 (ADEA)
   F. Vocational Rehabilitation Act of 1973
   G. Vietnam Era Veterans' Readjustment Assistance Act of 1974
   H. Pregnancy Discrimination Act of 1978 (PDA)
   I. Federal agency guidelines
      1. Uniform Guidelines on Employee Selection Procedures
      2. EEOC guidelines
   J. Sexual harassment
      1. Quid pro quo
      2. Hostile environment created by supervisors
   3. Hostile environment created by coworkers or non-employees

                a. Employers' responsibility
                b. *Meritor Savings Bank vs. Vinson*
            4. What the employer should do
                a. *Burlington Industries vs. Ellerth*
                b. *Faragher vs. City of Boca Raton*
                c. Reasonable care standard
                d. Steps to prevent sexual harassment claims
                    (1) Take all complaints seriously
                    (2) Issue strong policy statement condemning behavior
                    (3) Inform all employees about policy
                    (4) Develop complaint procedure
                    (5) Establish management response system for immediate action
                    (6) Conduct training sessions
                    (7) Discipline managers and employees
                    (8) Keep thorough records
                    (9) Conduct exit interviews
                    (10) Republish policy periodically
                    (11) Encourage upward communication
            5. What the employee can do
                a. File verbal complaint or protest with harasser and harasser's boss
                b. Write letter to accused
                c. If unwelcome conduct continues, file verbal and written report with harasser's manager and/or human resource director
                d. If unwelcome conduct still continues, contact EEOC
                e. Consult an attorney
        K. Selected early court decisions regarding equal employment opportunity
            1. *Griggs vs. Duke Power*
            2. *Albemarle Paper Company vs. Moody*
        L. Equal employment opportunity 1989-1991: A shifting Supreme Court
            1. *Price Waterhouse vs. Hopkins*
            2. *Wards Cove Packing Company vs. Atonio*

II. Equal Employment Opportunity 1991-Present
    A. The Civil Rights Act of 1991 (CRA 1991)
        1. Burden of proof (*Wards Cove*)
        2. Money damages
        3. Mixed motives (*Price-Waterhouse*)
        4. Proof of discrimination
    B. The Americans with Disabilities Act (ADA)
        1. Definition
            a. Reasonable accommodations
            b. Undue hardship
            c. Qualified individuals
            d. Essential functions
        2. ADA's legal obligations
        3. ADA in practice
    C. State and local equal employment opportunity laws
        1. Laws prohibiting employment discrimination that extend federal law
        2. Anti-bias laws
        3. State and local equal employment opportunity agencies

III. Defenses Against Discrimination Allegations
   A. What is adverse impact?
   B. How can adverse impact be proved?
      1. Disparate rejection rates
      2. Restricted policy
      3. Population comparisons
      4. *McDonnell-Douglas Test*
      5. Bringing a case of discrimination
   C. Bona fide occupational qualification (BFOQ)
      1. Age as a BFOQ
      2. Religion as a BFOQ
      3. Gender as a BFOQ
4. National origin as a BFOQ
   D. Business necessity
   E. Other considerations in discriminatory practice defenses
      1. Good intentions are no excuse
      2. Employers cannot count on hiding behind collective bargaining agreements
      3. A defense is not the only response to a charge of discrimination

IV. Illustrative Discriminatory Employment Practices
   A. What you can and cannot do
      1. Problem questions tend to identify applicants as members of protected group or adversely affect members of a protected group
      2. Questions become illegal if do screen out protected group members, no proof that practice is required as BFOQ or business necessity
   B. Discriminatory recruitment processes
      1. Word of mouth
      2. Misleading information
      3. Help wanted ads
   C. Discriminatory selection standards
      1. Educational requirements
      2. Tests
      3. Preference to relatives
      4. Height, weight and physical characteristics
      5. Arrest records
      6. Discharge due to garnishment
   D. Sample discriminatory promotion, transfer, and layoff practices
      1. Personal appearance regulations and Title VII
      2. Dress
      3. Grooming
      4. Hair
      5. Uniforms

V. The EEOC Enforcement Process
   A. Processing a charge
      1. Timing
      2. State, local, and federal EEOCs
      3. EEOC process
   B. Conciliation proceedings
      1. 30 days to work out conciliation agreement between parties
      2. EEOC conciliator meets with employee and then employer

3. Conciliation agreement reached, signed, and submitted to EEOC
4. If EEOC unable to obtain agreement, it may sue in federal district court
C. How to respond to employment discrimination charges
1. Investigating the charge
2. Fact-finding conference
D. The EEOC's determination and the attempted conciliation
E. Avoiding discrimination lawsuits with internal dispute resolution procedures
F. Mandatory arbitration of employment discrimination claims
1. *Gilmer vs. Interstate/Johnson Lane Corp.*
2. Compulsory arbitration

VI. Diversity Management and Affirmative Action Programs
A. Changing workforce demographics and globalization of markets
B. Managing diversity
1. Compulsory and voluntary activities
2. Provide strong leadership
3. Research: Assess the situation
4. Provide diversity training and education
5. Change culture and management systems
6. Evaluate the managing diversity program
C. Boosting work force diversity
D. Equal employment opportunity versus affirmative action
1. Equal employment opportunity - aims to ensure anyone gets equal chance for job based on qualifications regardless of race, color, sex, religion, national origin, or age
2. Affirmative action - requires employers to make extra effort to hire and promote those in the protected group
E. Steps in affirmative action program
1. Issue written equal employment policy
2. Appoint top official to oversee
3. Publicize policy and affirmative action commitment
4. Identify where affirmative action programs especially desirable
F. Affirmative action: Two basic strategies
1. Good faith effort strategy
2. Quota strategy
a. *Bakke vs. The Regents of the University of California* (1978)
b. *Wygant vs. Jackson Board of Education* (1986)
c. *Local 28 Sheet Metal Workers vs. EEOC* (1986)
d. *International Association of Firefighters vs. The City of Cleveland* (1986)
e. *U.S. vs. Paradise* (1987)
f. *Johnson vs. Transportation Agency, Santa Clara County* (1987)
3. Practical approach
a. Increase minority female applicant flow
b. Demonstrate top-management support for EEO policy
c. Demonstrate EEO commitment to community
d. Keep employees informed
e. Broaden work skills of incumbent employees
f. Internalize EEO policy to encourage supervisors' support

CHAPTER STUDY QUIZZES

Match Terms With Definitions

a. Title VII of the 1964 Civil Rights Act
b. *Albemarle Paper Company v. Moody*
c. hostile environment harassment
d. *Wards Cove v. Atonio*
e. adverse impact
f. affirmative action
g. protected class
h. disparate treatment
i. quid pro quo harassment
j. bona fide occupational qualification

_____ 1. The law that states that an employer cannot discriminate on the basis of race, color, religion, sex, or national origin in making employment decisions.

_____ 2. Steps that are taken for the purpose of eliminating the present effects of past discrimination.

_____ 3. Harassment on the basis of sex that has the purpose or effect of substantially interfering with a person's work performance by requiring sexual favors in exchange for employment rewards.

_____ 4. Harassment on the basis of sex that has the purpose or effect of creating an intimidating or offensive work environment.

_____ 5. Persons, such as minorities and women, protected by equal opportunity laws.

_____ 6. Supreme Court case in which it was ruled that the validity of job tests must be documented and that employee performance standards must be unambiguous.

_____ 7. Intentional discrimination on the basis of a protected class.

_____ 8. Supreme Court case in which the decision made it difficult to prove a case of unlawful discrimination against an employer.

_____ 9. The overall impact of employer practices that result in significantly higher percentages of members of minorities and other protected groups being rejected for employment, placement, or promotion.

_____ 10. Requirement that an employee be of a certain religion, sex, or national origin where that is reasonably necessary to the organization's normal operation.

True/False

1. T F Title VII states that an employer cannot discriminate on the basis of race, color, age and disability.

2. T F The Equal Employment Opportunity Commission is the enforcement agency for Title VII.

3. T F The Age Discrimination in Employment Act makes it unlawful to discriminate against employees between the ages of 40 and 65.

4. T F Sexual harassment only exists if the advances are made by the supervisor to the employee.

5. T F   The ADA requires that employers provide reasonable accommodation for qualified individuals with disabilities.

6. T F   Adverse impact results when an employer intentionally discriminates against members of a protected classification.

7. T F   National origin can never be used as a BFOQ.

8. T F   Physical requirements that have an adverse impact on protected groups but that can be proven to be job related are allowed by law.

9. T F   Arrest records are acceptable to use in employment screening.

10. T F   Many employers are switching to compulsory mandatory arbitration.

11. T F   Affirmative action is the same thing as equal employment opportunity.

12. T F   Reverse discrimination involves discrimination against male non-minority persons.

Multiple Choice

1. Title VII of the 1964 Civil Rights Act states that an employer cannot discriminate on the basis of
    a. race, color, religion, sex, or national origin.
    b. race, age, religion, sex, or disability.
    c. age, color, race, religion, sex, or national orgin.
    d. disability, race, religion, sex, or age.

2. The enforcement agency responsible for ensuring compliance with executive orders is the
    a. Equal Employment Opportunity Commission.
    b. Department of Labor.
    c. Department of Human Resources.
    d. Office of Federal Contract Compliance Programs.

3. According to the Equal Pay Act, it is unlawful to discriminate in pay on the basis of sex when jobs involve
    a. comparable work, similar skills, effort, and responsibility.
    b. equal work, equivalent skills, effort, and responsibility.
    c. comparable work, equivalent skills, effort, and responsibility.
    d. equal work, similar skills, effort, and responsibility.

4. The Vocational Rehabilitation Act of 1973 requires which employers to take affirmative action for the employment of handicapped persons?
    a. all employers
    b. all employers with federal contracts
    c. employers with federal contracts over $2,500
    d. employers with more than 15 employees

5. Which of the following is true about the Pregnancy Discrimination Act?
    a. If an employer offers its employees disability coverage, then pregnancy and childbirth must be treated like any other disability and included as a covered condition in the plan.
    b. Pregnancy, childbirth, or related medical conditions cannot be used as a factor in the hiring, promotion, suspension, or discharge of an individual.
    c. The employer can decide whether or not to provide disability and other insurance coverage to pregnant employees.
    d. both a and b

6. The purpose of the Uniform Guidelines on Employee Selection Procedures is to provide
    a. detailed information about exactly how an employer should go about hiring an employee.
    b. highly recommended procedures for such matters as employee selection and record keeping.
    c. loose guidelines for such matters as employee selection.
    d. general information about where to find employees.

7. John was Tatiana's immediate supervisor. He would often come up behind her while she was working and rub her neck and make comments about her body. Tatiana has repeatedly asked him to stop these behaviors. Based on this information, Tatiana probably can make a good case for which type of sexual harassment?
    a. quid pro quo
    b. gender discrimination
    c. mixed motive discrimination
    d. hostile environment harassment

8. Which of the following is one way that an organization can minimize its liability if a sexual harassment claim is filed against the organization?
    a. terminate the offending party
    b. terminate the person making the claim
    c. take the complaint seriously and conduct an investigation
    d. call in both parties and have them discuss the allegations with you at the same time

9. The landmark Supreme Court case that defined unfair discrimination was
    a. *Albemarle Paper Company v. Moody.*
    b. *Griggs v. Duke Power Company.*
    c. *Wards Cove Packing Company v. Atonio.*
    d. *Price Waterhouse v. Hopkins.*

10. Which of the following was not a main provision of the Civil Rights Act of 1991?
    a. reaffirmed that the burden of proof is on the employer to show that an employment practice is required as a business necessity
    b. removes the option for employers to avoid liability by proving that it would have taken the same action even without the discriminatory motive
    c. eliminates option for employers to "adjust" test scores to be more inclusive of minorities
    d. defined what is covered under the Equal Pay Act

11. Redesigning a job so that a qualified person with a disability can perform the job is known as
    a. reasonable accommodation.
    b. undue hardship.
    c. business necessity.
    d. bona fide occupational qualification.

12. The McDonnell-Douglas Test can be used to prove
    a. disparate treatment.
    b. sexual harassment.
    c. undue hardship.
    d. adverse impact.

13. If the EEOC issues a cause finding in a discrimination case, what is the next step in the process of resolving the situation?
    a. the case automatically goes to court
    b. the employer has to pay an immediate settlement, at its discretion
    c. the EEOC has 30 days to work out a conciliation agreement between the parties
    d. the case is remanded to the OFCCP

14. Managing diversity in an organization is concerned with
    a. maximizing potential advantages of diversity while minimizing potential barriers to diversity.
    b. only maximizing potential advantages of diversity.
    c. only minimizing potential barriers to diversity.
    d. setting affirmative action quotas.

15. The main difference between equal employment opportunity and affirmative action is that
    a. affirmative action goes beyond equal employment opportunity by requiring employers to make an extra effort to hire and promote members of protected groups.
    b. equal employment opportunity goes beyond affirmative action by requiring employers to make an extra effort to hire and promote members of protected groups.
    c. equal employment opportunity is not required while affirmative action is required.
    d. There is no difference between the two.

Essays

1. What is the purpose of equal employment opportunity laws such at Title VII of the 1964 Civil Rights Act, the ADEA, etc.?

2. Identify the steps that an employer can take to reduce both the likelihood of sexual harassment occurring in the workplace and its liability should such harassment occur.

3. What is adverse impact and how can it be proven?

4. Discuss why managing diversity is important for organizations.

5. Compare and contrast an affirmative action strategy focusing on good faith effort with a quota strategy.

ANSWER KEY

Match Terms with Definitions

1. a (p. 37)
2. f (p. 38)
3. i (p. 42)
4. c (p. 40)
5. g (p. 45)
6. b (p. 45)
7. h (p. 53)
8. d (p. 46)
9. e (p. 51)
10. j (p. 54)

True/False

1. F (p. 37)
2. T (p. 38)
3. F (p. 38)
4. F (p. 42)
5. T (p. 49)
6. F (p. 51)
7. F (p. 55)
8. T (p. 58)
9. F (p. 58)
10. T (p. 64)
11. F (p. 68)
12. T (p. 70)

Multiple Choice

1. a   (p. 37)
2. d   (p. 38)
3. b   (p. 38)
4. c   (p. 39)
5. d   (p. 39)

6. b   (p. 40)
7. d   (p. 42)
8. c   (p. 43)
9. b   (p. 45)
10. d   (p. 47)

11. a   (p. 49)
12. a   (p. 53)
13. c   (p. 63)
14. a   (p. 66)
15. a   (p. 68)

Essay

1. Pages 37-39
2. Pages 40-44
3. Pages 51-54
4. Pages 66-68
5. Page 69

CHAPTER 3

JOB ANALYSIS

CHAPTER DESCRIPTION

This chapter describes the importance of the job analysis process, the methods available to conduct a job analysis, and how to write a job description. The chapter also discusses the role of job analysis in a "dejobbed" world.

CHAPTER OBJECTIVES

1. Describe the basic methods of collecting job analysis information.
2. Discuss how to conduct a job analysis.
3. Demonstrate the process of writing a job description.
4. Explain the purpose of a job specification and a procedure for developing one.

CHAPTER STUDY OUTLINE

I. The Nature of Job Analysis
   A. Job analysis defined
      1. Work activities
      2. Human behaviors
      3. Machines, tools, equipment, and work aids used
      4. Performance standards
      5. Job context
      6. Human requirements
   B. Uses of job analysis information
      1. Recruitment and selection
      2. Compensation
      3. Performance appraisal
      4. Training
      5. Ensuring complete assignment of duties
   C. Steps in job analysis
      1. Identify how information will be used
      2. Review relevant background information
          a. Process chart shows work flow
          b. Existing job description provides starting point for revision
      3. Select representative position to be analyzed
      4. Analyze the job
      5. Review information from job incumbents
      6. Develop job description and job specification

II. Methods of Collecting Job Analysis Information
   A. The interview
      1. Pros and cons
      2. Typical questions
      3. Interview guidelines
          a. Job analyst and supervisor should work together
          b. Establish rapport quickly
          c. Follow structured guide or checklist
          d. Ask for order of importance and frequency of occurrence of nonroutine tasks
          e. Review and verify data
   B. Questionnaires
   C. Observation

    D. Participant diary/logs
    E. U. S. Civil Service Procedure
    F. Quantitative job analysis techniques
        1. Position Analysis Questionnaire
        2. Department of Labor (DOL) Procedure
        3. Functional Job Analysis
    G. Obtain multiple perspectives

III. Writing Job Descriptions
    A. Job identification
        1. Job title
        2. Job status
        3. Date
        4. Person approving description
        5. Supervisor's title
        6. Job salary/pay scale
        7. Grade/level
    B. Job summary
    C. Relationships
        1. Reports to
        2. Supervises
        3. Works with
        4. Outside the company
    D. Responsibilities and duties
    E. Standards of performance
    F. Working conditions and physical environment
    G. Job description guidelines
        1. Writing job descriptions
            a. Be clear
            b. Indicate scope of authority
            c. Be specific
            d. Be brief
            e. Recheck
        2. Complying with ADA
        3. Identifying essential job functions

IV. Writing Job Specifications
    A. Specifications for trained versus untrained personnel
    B. Job specifications based on judgment
    C. Job specifications based on statistical analysis
        1. Steps in statistical process
            a. Analyze job and decide how to measure performance
            b. Select personal traits that should predict successful performance
            c. Test candidates for these traits
            d. Measure subsequent job performance
            e. Statistically analyze the relationship between human trait and job performance
        2. Personality-related job requirements

V. Job Analysis in a "Jobless" World
    A. From specialized to enlarged jobs
        1. Jobs
        2. Job enlargement
        3. Job enrichment
            a. Form natural work groups
            b. Combine tasks
            c. Establish client relationships

d.	Vertical loading
		e.	Open feedback channels
	B.	Becoming de-jobbed: The need for competitiveness
		1.	Flatter organizations
		2.	Work teams
		3.	Boundaryless organization
		4.	Reengineering
		5.	Future of job descriptions

CHAPTER STUDY QUIZZES

Match Terms with Definitions

a.	job description
b.	essential job functions
c.	job enrichment
d.	reengineering
e.	participant diary

f.	job specifications
g.	job enlargement
h.	boundaryless organization
i.	job identification
j.	job rotation

_____	1.	Redesigning jobs in a way that increases the opportunities for the worker to experience feelings of responsibility, achievement, growth, and recognition.

_____	2.	A list of what the job entails.

_____	3.	A list of a job's human requirements, or what kind of people to hire for the job.

_____	4.	Job duties that employees must be able to perform, with or without reasonable accommodation.

_____	5.	Assigning workers additional same-level activities, thus increasing the number of activities they perform.

_____	6.	An organization in which widespread use of teams and similar structural mechanisms means that the hierarchical levels are reduced and made more permeable.

_____	7.	The fundamental rethinking and radical redesign of business processes to achieve dramatic improvement in critical measures of performance.

_____	8.	Job analysis data collected by having workers keep a list of what they do during the day.

_____	9.	A section of a job description that contains job title, supervisor's title, and grade/level of the job.

_____	10.	Systematically moving workers from one job to another.

True/False

1.	T	F	Job analysis information is essential for estimating the value of and appropriate compensation for jobs.

2.	T	F	Job context refers to information about the human requirements of the job.

3.	T	F	Job analysis information should only be evaluated with the immediate supervisor of the job incumbent.

4. T F A process chart is the same as an organization chart.

5. T F A job analysis questionnaire is a quick and efficient way to obtain information from a large number of employees.

6. T F Order of importance and frequency of occurrence of work tasks is critical information about non-routine tasks.

7. T F The U. S. Civil Service job analysis process is an unstructured procedure for comparing different jobs.

8. T F Only one source of job analysis information is sufficient.

9. T F A job description is a written statement of what the jobholder does, how he or she does it, and under what conditions the job is performed.

10. T F The job summary on a job description should include a detailed listing of all job duties.

11. T F The judgmental approach to writing job specifications is used by trained job analysis personnel.

12. T F Until recently, a job was defined as a set of closely related activities carried out for pay.

Multiple Choice

1. The steps in conducting a job analysis include all but which of the following?
    a. identifying the use to which the information will be put
    b. selecting representative positions to be analyzed
    c. reviewing the information with job incumbents
    d. analyzing all jobs in the organization

2. The most widely used method of determining a job's duties and responsibilities is the
    a. interview.
    b. videotaping.
    c. essay.
    d. observation.

3. When jobs consist mainly of observable physical activity, an especially useful method for collecting job analysis information is
    a. an interview.
    b. a questionnaire.
    c. observation.
    d. a participant diary.

4. An advantage of using the Position Analysis Questionnaire (PAQ) to collect job analysis information is that it
    a. is a qualitative job analysis technique.
    b. provides a quantitative score or profile of any job in terms of how that job rates on five basic job activities.
    c. only involves a few people.
    d. is very inexpensive.

5. The Department of Labor job analysis procedure classifies jobs in terms of
   a. people, data, and things.
   b. data, things, and risk.
   c. effort, knowledge, and skills.
   d. people, knowledge, and things.

6. The method of job analysis based on the Department of Labor method is the
   a. Position Analysis Questionnaire.
   b. Observation by Videotaping.
   c. Labor Interview Technique.
   d. Functional Job Analysis.

7. Job descriptions typically include all but which of the following types of information?
   a. job identification
   b. incumbent's name
   c. job summary
   d. authority of incumbent

8. A job description can best be described as a
   a. written statement of what the jobholder brings to the job in terms of knowledge, skills, and abilities.
   b. written statement of what the jobholder actually does, how he or she does it, and under what conditions the job is performed.
   c. written contract between the employer and employee regarding what the employee will do on the job.
   d. verbal description of the job provided to the employee at the time he or she is hired

9. Well-written job descriptions follow all but which of these guidelines?
   a. clear
   b. indicate scope of authority
   c. brief
   d. general

10. The Americans with Disabilities Act (ADA) requires that employment decisions be based on
    a. all job duties, tasks, and responsibilities.
    b. only essential functions of the job.
    c. whatever the employer deems appropriate.
    d. only the five most important tasks and functions.

11. What is the primary difference between writing job specifications for trained versus untrained personnel?
    a. Job specifications for trained employees are harder to write because of the complexity of the job.
    b. Job specifications for untrained employees are easier to write because the jobs are not complex.
    c. Job specifications for trained employees are relatively straightforward while job specifications for untrained personnel are more complex.
    d. There is no difference in writing job specifications for these two groups.

12. Research has shown that which of the following work behaviors are generic across jobs?
    a. thoroughness, industriousness, and attendance
    b. industriousness, attendance, and conscientiousness
    c. analytical skills, off-task behavior, and conscientiousness
    d. thoroughness, attendance, and analytical skills

13. Basing a job analysis on statistical analysis is primarily concerned with determining the relationship between
    a. two criteria of job effectiveness.
    b. two predictors of job effectiveness.
    c. some predictor and some measure of skill.
    d. some predictor and some criterion of job effectiveness

14. Job enrichment can result from doing all but which of the following?
    a. forming natural work groups
    b. separating tasks
    c. vertical loading
    d. establishing client relationships

15. De-jobbing is resulting primarily from
    a. a lack of motivation on the part of workers.
    b. apathy on the part of management.
    c. changes taking place in business such as globalization and technology.
    d. more hierarchical organizations.

Essays

1. Discuss why job analysis is critical to human resource management.

2. What are the six steps in conducting a job analysis?

3. Compare and contrast qualitative versus quantitative methods of job analysis.

4. Describe the various components of a job description, indicating why each is important to include.

5. Discuss what it means for a company to become dejobbed.

ANSWER KEY

Match Terms with Definitions

1. c   (p. 110)
2. a   (p. 84)
3. f   (p. 84)
4. b   (p. 103)
5. g   (p. 110)
6. h   (p. 111)
7. d   (p. 111)
8. e   (p. 92)
9. i   (p. 99)
10. j   (p. 110)

True/False

1. T   (p. 84)
2. F   (p. 84)
3. F   (p. 86)
4. F   (p. 86)
5. T   (p. 91)
6. T   (p. 91)
7. F   (p. 92)
8. F   (p. 97)
9. T   (p. 98)
10. F   (p. 99)
11. F   (p. 107)
12. T   (p. 109)

Multiple Choice

1. d   (p. 85-87)
2. a   (p. 88)
3. c   (p. 91)
4. b   (p. 94)
5. a   (p. 94)
6. d   (p. 97)
7. b   (p. 98)
8. b   (p. 102-103)
9. d   (p. 98)
10. b   (p. 102)
11. c   (p. 107)
12. a   (p. 108)
13. d   (p. 109)
14. b   (p. 110)
15. c   (p. 110)

Essay

1. Pages 84-85
2. Pages 85-87
3. Pages 87-97
4. Pages 98-103
5. Pages 110-112

CHAPTER 4

PERSONNEL PLANNING AND RECRUITMENT

CHAPTER DESCRIPTION

This chapter describes the process of planning for human resource needs within organizations as well as how to recruit prospective employees to fill those needs.

CHAPTER OBJECTIVES

1. Explain the process of forecasting personnel requirements.
2. Discuss the pros and cons of eight methods used for recruiting job candidates.
3. Describe how to develop an application form.
4. Explain how to use application forms to predict job performance.

CHAPTER STUDY OUTLINE

I. The Recruitment and Selection Process
   A. First step is personnel planning
   B. Recruiting process is series of hurdles

II. Employment Planning and Forecasting
   A. Employment planning
      1. Process of formulating plans to fill or eliminate future openings
      2. Based on analysis of the positions expected to be open and needed
      3. Uses information about internal and external candidate availability
      4. Integral part of firm's strategic plan
   B. How to forecast personnel needs
      1. Trend analysis
      2. Ratio analysis
      3. Scatter plot
      4. Computerized forecasts
      5. Managerial judgment
   C. Forecasting the supply of inside candidates
      1. Qualifications inventories
         a. Manual systems
            (1) Personnel replacement charts
            (2) Position replacement charts
         b. Computerized information systems
      2. Privacy issues
   D. Internal sources of candidates
      1. Job posting
      2. Computerized systems
      3. Personnel records
      4. Rehiring former employees
      5. Succession planning
   E. Forecasting the supply of outside candidates
      1. Forecast general economic conditions and expected prevailing rate of unemployment
         a. Published economic forecasts
         b. Local labor market conditions
      2. Forecast availability of potential job candidates in specific occupations for which you will be recruiting

III. Recruiting Job Candidates
   A. Overview of recruitment issues
      1. Develop an applicant pool using internal and external recruitment activities
      2. Use recruiting yield pyramid to calculate number of applicants that must be generated to hire required number of new employees
   B. Advertising as a source of candidates
      1. Principles of help wanted advertising
         a. Create interest in the job
         b. Prompt action
      2. Must comply with various employment laws
   C. Employment agencies as a source of candidates
      1. Type of employment agencies
         a. Public agencies operated by federal, state, or local governments
         b. Agencies associated with nonprofit organizations
         c. Privately owned agencies
         d. Reasons to use agencies
      2. Using temporary help agencies
         a. Used to find contingent or temporary workers
         b. No longer limited to clerical or maintenance staff
      3. Guidelines for employers to boost likelihood that relationships with temporary workers will be mutually beneficial
         a. Provide honest information about length of assignment
         b. Ensure fair and respectful treatment
         c. Use independent contractors and permanent part-time employees
         d. Consider impact on full-time workers
         e. Provide necessary training and orientation
         f. Beware of legal issues
         g. Provide policies for:
            (1) Invoicing
            (2) Time sheets
            (3) Temp-to-perm policy
            (4) Recruitment of and benefits for temp employees
            (5) Inside staff
            (6) Dress code
            (7) Equal employment opportunity statement
            (8) Job description information
   D. Alternative staffing techniques
      1. Traditional temporary help
      2. Long-term temporary assignments
      3. Master vendor arrangements
      4. In-house temporary employees
      5. Payrolling
      6. Part-time employees
      7. Independent contractors
      8. Contract technical workers
      9. Employee leasing
      10. Outsourcing or managed services
      11. Temp-to-perm programs
      12. Temp-to-lease programs
   E. Executive recruiters – headhunters
      1. Special employment agencies retained by company
      2. Focus on top-management talent for clients
   F. College recruiting as source of candidates

1. Important source of management trainees, promotable candidates, and professional and technical employees
2. Relatively expensive
3. Time consuming for the recruiters
4. Internships
- G. Referrals and walk-ins as a source of candidates
   1. Employee referral campaigns
   2. Walk-ins – direct applications
- H. Recruiting on the internet
   1. Cost effective
   2. More timely
   3. Downside may be flood of responses
- I. Recruiting a more diverse workforce
   1. Older workers
   2. Minorities and women
   3. Welfare-to-work programs
- J. Other recruiting sources
   1. Moonlighters
   2. Retired or exiting military personnel
   3. Disabled individuals
- K. Recruiting methods used determined by type of job

IV. Developing and Using Application Forms
- A. Purpose of application forms
   1. Provides information for making judgments on substantive matters
   2. Can draw conclusions about applicant's previous progress and growth
   3. Can draw tentative conclusions regarding applicant's stability
   4. Provides data to predict which candidates will succeed on the job
- B. Equal opportunity and application forms
   1. Ensure forms comply with equal employment laws
   2. Mandatory dispute resolution forms may be part of process
- C. Using application forms to predict job performance
   1. Job tenure
   2. Employee theft

CHAPTER STUDY QUIZZES

Match Terms with Definitions

a. employment planning
b. scatter plot
c. qualifications inventories
d. job posting
e. public employment agencies
f. ratio analysis
g. private employment agencies
h. trend analysis
i. outsourcing
j. employee leasing

_____ 1. Making forecasts based on the ratio between some causal factor and the number of employees required.

_____ 2. Studying firm's employment levels over past five years or so to predict future needs.

_____ 3. Summary data about employees such as performance record, educational background, and promotability.

_____ 4. The process of formulating plans to fill or eliminate future openings, based on an analysis of positions expected to be needed and whether candidates will be internal or external.

_____ 5. Publicizing open jobs to current employees.

_____ 6. Agencies that charge fees for applicants who are placed.

_____ 7. When an independent company with expertise in operating a specific function contracts with a client company to take full operational responsibility for performing that function.

_____ 8. Agencies supported by the U. S. Department of Labor to provide employment services to individuals and companies.

_____ 9. When a company transfers employees to the payroll of another company that leases the workers back to the client company and administers the payroll, provides benefits and benefits administration and other personnel activities normally handled by an HR department.

_____ 10. A graphic way to show the relationship between a measure of business activity and staffing levels.

True/False

1. T F Personnel planning is the first step in the recruiting and selecting process.

2. T F Succession planning is the process of planning to fill all jobs in the organization.

3. T F Trend analysis involves making forecasts based on the ratio between some causal factor and number of employees required.

4. T F A personnel replacement chart tracks inside candidates for important positions.

5. T F Privacy issues are not important to consider when planning for human resource needs.

6. T F Job posting is an external source of job candidates.

7. T F One factor to consider when forecasting the supply of outside candidates is the occupational market conditions.

8. T F The effectiveness of the firm's recruiting process has a big impact on candidates' opinions of the firm.

9. T F Use of employment agencies can reduce the number of interviews the company has to conduct.

10. T F One of the best ways to utilize employment agencies is to use as many as possible.

11. T F Contingent workers may be more productive and less expensive to recruit and train than permanent workers.

12. T F One advantage to internet recruiting is the lower cost than advertising in media such as newspapers.

Multiple Choice

1. An assumption of both trend analysis and ratio analysis is that
   a. productivity remains about the same.
   b. productivity changes quarterly.
   c. productivity always increases.

d. productivity always decreases.

2. One advantage of using computerized forecasting is the ability to
   a. have data entered quickly and, thus, minimize the cost of having forecasts done.
   b. quickly translate projected productivity and sales levels into forecasts of personnel needs while estimating the effects of various productivity and sales levels on personnel requirements.
   c. maintain an inventory of applicants for various jobs and various locations.
   d. ensure that forecasts won't change since they have been estimated by a computer.

3. The purpose of personnel replacement charts is to
   a. ensure that all levels of employees have backups.
   b. to keep track of inside candidates for the most important positions.
   c. make personnel's job easier.
   d. let supervisors pick and choice whom they want working for them.

4. Which of the following is not a concern regarding privacy and human resource planning?
   a. who has access to the data
   b. how data is identified
   c. what data is legally protected
   d. which type of software to use

5. Jim applied for a promotion within the company but didn't get it. Which of the following might be his reaction, and is one of the problems with hiring from within?
   a. He may become discontented with the company.
   b. He may be relieved that he doesn't have to do the extra work.
   c. He may just assume he wasn't qualified.
   d. He probably won't react at all.

6. Juanita left her high tech job at Baker Electronics to take a job with a competitor. She has now been offered a job back at Baker. What is a concern over rehiring former employees?
   a. what it may signal to current employees – that the best way to get ahead in the firm is to leave and return
   b. whether or not they have the skills to do the job
   c. how well they remember their old job
   d. there should be no concerns with this practice

7. The plan companies make to fill the most important executive positions is known as
   a. replacement progress.
   b. executive planning.
   c. succession planning.
   d. occupational mapping.

8. The process used to calculate the number of applicants the organization must generate to hire the required number of new employees is known as a
   a. recruiting yardstick plan.
   b. recruiting strategy plan.
   c. recruiting pentagon.
   d. recruiting yield pyramid.

9. A good help wanted ad will do all but which of the following?
   a. get people interested in the job
   b. prompt action
   c. inhibit qualified responses
   d. create desire for the job

10. If a job is listed as "fee-paid" with an employment agency, this means
    a. the applicant has to pay a fee to the agency.
    b. the employer has to pay a fee to the agency.
    c. the applicant has to pay a fee to the employer.
    d. the agency has to pay the employer a fee.

11. Self-employed persons whose services are engaged on a contract basis and who are hired to perform specialized tasks generally requiring a high level of independence, judgment, skill, and discretion, are known as
    a. long-term temporary help.
    b. master vendors.
    c. leased employees.
    d. independent contractors.

12. An advantage of using a headhunter to find executive talent is that the headhunter
    a. is not very expensive.
    b. has many contacts and is adept at contacting qualified candidates.
    c. works just for the company.
    d. will intuitively understand the type of employee needed.

13. College recruiting has two goals:
    a. (1) finding and screening candidates and (2) attracting them to the company.
    b. (1) screening candidates and (2) selecting candidates.
    c. (1) finding and screening candidates and (2) selecting candidates.
    d. (1) finding candidates and (2) attracting all of them to the company.

14. Which of the following is potentially a discriminatory question to include on an application form?
    a. Have you ever been arrested?
    b. What is your full name?
    c. Who is your current employer?
    d. What is your telephone number?

15. Application forms can help the employer determine which candidate(s)
    a. is absolutely the most qualified.
    b. appear to be the best match for the job based on reported qualifications.
    c. will have the best fit with the culture.
    d. should be sent for drug testing.

Essays

1. Discuss why forecasting personnel needs is critical to organizational effectiveness.

2. What are the advantages and disadvantages of hiring internal versus external candidates?

3. Briefly describe the various methods that can be used to source candidates for open positions.

4. When might an organization want to use an employment agency for assistance with staffing?

5. Why would a firm consider alternative staffing options?

ANSWER KEY

Match Terms with Definitions

1. f (p. 123)   6. g (p. 138)
2. h (p. 123)   7. i (p. 145)

3. c   (p. 125)
4. a   (p. 122)
5. d   (p. 130)

8. e   (p. 136-137)
9. j   (p. 145)
10. b (p. 124)

True/False

1. T   (p. 122)
2. F   (p. 122)
3. F   (p. 123)
4. T   (p. 125)

5. F   (p. 128)
6. F   (p. 130)
7. T   (p. 132)
8. T   (p. 134)

9. T   (p. 139)
10. F (p. 141)
11. T (p. 142)
12. T (p. 153)

Multiple Choice

1. a   (p. 123)
2. b   (p. 125)
3. b   (p. 125)
4. d   (p. 128)
5. a   (p. 130)

6. a   (p. 130-131)
7. c   (p. 132)
8. d   (p. 133)
9. c   (p. 135)
10. b (p. 138)

11. d (p. 145)
12. b (p. 146)
13. a (p. 150)
14. a (p. 160)
15. b (p. 159)

Essay

1. Pages 123-128
2. Pages 130
3. Pages 133+
4. Pages 138
5. Pages 144-145

CHAPTER 5

EMPLOYEE TESTING AND SELECTION

CHAPTER DESCRIPTION

This chapter discusses the importance of a well-constructed selection process, describes procedures for developing and implementing such a process, and reviews various selection techniques commonly used in organizations.

CHAPTER OBJECTIVES

1. Describe the overall selection process and explain why it is important.
2. Define basic testing concepts including validity and reliability.
3. Discuss at least four types of personnel tests.
4. Explain the pros and cons of background investigations, reference checks, and pre-employment information services.

CHAPTER STUDY OUTLINE

I. The Selection Process
   A. Why careful selection is important
      1. Your own performance depends in part on your subordinates' performance
      2. Costs associated with recruiting and hiring employees
   B. Legal implications and negligent hiring
      1. Avoiding discrimination against protected groups
      2. Avoiding liability from negligent hiring
         a. *Ponticas v. K.M.S. Investments*
         b. *Henley v. Prince Georges County*

II. Basic Testing Concepts
   A. Validity answers the question: "Does this test measure what it's supposed to measure?"
      1. Criterion validity – demonstrating that those who do well on the test also do well on the job and vice versa
         a. Predictor – the measurement that you are trying to relate to a criterion
         b. Criterion – the measure of job success such as performance on the job
      2. Content validity – demonstrating that the test constitutes a fair sample of the content of the job
         a. Identify behaviors critical to performance
         b. Randomly select a sample of those tasks and behaviors for the tests
   B. Reliability refers to test's consistency
      1. Retest estimate – administer the same test to same people at two points in time
      2. Equivalent form estimate – administer two comparable (equivalent) tests
      3. Internal consistency – administer the test and statistically analyze the degree to which responses to items vary together
      4. Sources of unreliability
         a. Questions may do poor job of sampling material
         b. Errors due to chance response tendencies
         c. Errors due to changes in testing conditions
         d. Changes in the person taking the test (e.g., learning, memory)
   C. How to validate a test
      1. Analyze the job
      2. Choose your tests
      3. Administer tests

        4. Relate test scores and criteria
        5. Cross-validate and revalidate
    D. Testing guidelines
        1. Use tests as supplements
        2. Validate the tests
        3. Analyze all current hiring and promotion standards
        4. Keep accurate records
        5. Begin validation program now
        6. Use certified psychologist
        7. Test conditions are important

III. Ethical, Legal, and Fairness Questions in Testing
    A. Equal employment opportunity aspects of testing
        1. Must prove that tests are related to success or failure on the job
        2. Must prove that tests don't unfairly discriminate against either minority or nonminority subgroups
    B. Alternatives if adverse impact present
        1. Choose an alternative selection procedure that does not have adverse impact
        2. Show that test is valid predictor of performance on the job
        3. Monitor the selection test to see whether it has disparate impact
    C. Rights of test takers and test security
        1. Right to confidentiality of test results and right to informed consent regarding use of results
        2. Right to expect that only qualified personnel will have access to scores
        3. Right to expect that test is equally fair to all test takers
    D. HR Research
        1. Face validity important for perceptions of fairness
        2. Belief that employer had right to obtain information with a particular technique
        3. Extent to which procedure is widely used in industry
    E. Privacy
        1. U. S. Supreme Court decisions
        2. Federal Privacy Act
        3. Common law of torts

IV. Types of Tests
    A. Tests of cognitive ability
        1. Intelligence tests
        2. Specific cognitive abilities—aptitude tests
    B. Tests of motor and physical abilities
    C. Tests of personality and interests
        1. Projective tests
        2. Personality inventories
        3. Interest inventories
    D. Achievement tests

V. Work Samples and Simulations
    A. Rationale—measures how a candidate actually performs some of a job's basic tasks
    B. Developing a work sampling procedure
        1. List all possible tasks
        2. Break tasks down into steps needed to complete them
        3. Validate by determining relationship between applicants' scores on work samples and actual performance on job
        4. Begin using test
    C. Management assessment centers
    D. Video-based situational testing
    E. Miniature job training and evaluation approach

VI. Other Selection Techniques
   A. Background investigations and reference checks
      1. To verify accuracy of factual information provided by applicant
      2. To discover damaging background information such as criminal records
      3. Inexpensive and straightforward way to verify factual information
      4. Laws that affect references
         a. Privacy Act of 1974
         b. Fair Credit Reporting Act of 1970
         c. Family Education Rights and Privacy Act of 1974 (and Buckley Amendment of 1974)
         d. Freedom of Information Act of 1966
      5. Guidelines for giving references
      6. Reemployment information services
   B. Polygraph and honesty testing
      1. Paper-and-pencil tests
      2. Honesty screening program
   C. Graphology
   D. Physical examination
   E. Drug screening
   F. Testing, selection, and organizational performance
   G. Complying with the Immigration Reform and Control Act of 1986

CHAPTER STUDY QUIZZES

Match Terms with Definitions

a. expectancy chart
b. reliability
c. achievement tests
d. interest inventories
e. motor abilities

f. content validity
g. cognitive tests
h. personality tests
i. reference check
j. criterion validity

_____ 1. Demonstrating that those who do well on a test also do well on the job and that those who do poorly on the test do poorly on the job.

_____ 2. Consistency of a test.

_____ 3. Demonstrating that a test constitutes a fair sample of the content of the job.

_____ 4. Graphic representation of the relationship between a test and job performance.

_____ 5. Finger dexterity, manual dexterity, speed of arm movement, and reaction time.

_____ 6. Comparison of one's interests with those of people in various occupations.

_____ 7. Instruments that measure attributes such as extroversion, stability, and motivation.

_____ 8. Measure of what a person has learned.

_____ 9. Measure of general reasoning ability.

_____ 10. Verification of job applicant's background.

True/False

1. T F   One reason selection is so important is that your performance as a manager always depends in part on the performance of your subordinates.

2. T F   Employers cannot be held liable for criminal activities of employees regardless of whether or not they conduct pre-employment background checks.

3. T F   Test reliability answers the question: "Does this test measure what it is supposed to measure?"

4. T F   One source of test unreliability results from errors due to changes in testing conditions such as noisy rooms.

5. T F   Face validity results when there is an obvious link between the selection procedure and performing the job.

6. T F   Intelligence tests are tests of specific cognitive abilities.

7. T F   Conscientiousness, one of the "big five" personality dimensions has been found to have a consistent relationship with all job performance criteria for all occupations studied.

8. T F   A management assessment center only measures how an applicant actually performs some of a job's basic tasks.

9. T F   The most commonly used form of background check is a full background check including credit history.

10. T F   Paper-and-pencil honesty tests are psychological tests designed to predict job applicants' proneness to dishonesty and other forms of counterproductivity.

11. T F   The most common use of drug testing is to test job candidates just before they are formally hired.

12. T F   Under the Immigration Reform and Control Act of 1986, a person has to be a U. S. citizen to be employed.

Multiple Choice

1. Demonstrating that the tasks the person performs on a test of management skills is in fact a comprehensive and random sample of the tasks performed on the job of manager requires evidence of
    a. criterion validity.
    b. reliability.
    c. content validity.
    d. construct validity.

2. Which of the following is not a form of estimating test reliability?
    a. retest estimate
    b. internal consistency
    c. scaled back estimate
    d. equivalent form estimate

3. Administering a test to a group of employees and then comparing their scores with their current performance is an example of which type of test validation?
    a. predictive validation
    b. concurrent validation
    c. content validation
    d. construct validation

4. If a job applicant claims that a selection test used by your organization has adverse impact, which of the following alternatives would not be a good solution?
    a. continue to use the test
    b. choose an alternative procedure that does not have an adverse impact
    c. show that the test is valid
    d. monitor the selection test to see whether it has adverse impact

5. According to the American Psychological Association's standard for educational and psychological tests, test takers have which of the following rights?
    a. the right to confidentiality of test results and the right to informed consent regarding the use of test results
    b. the right to expect that only people qualified to interpret the scores will have access to them or that sufficient information will accompany the scores to ensure their appropriate interpretation
    c. the right to expect that the test is equally fair to all test takers in the sense of being equally familiar
    d. all of the above

6. The type of general tests that measure a range of abilities including memory, vocabulary, verbal fluency, and numerical ability are known as
    a. intelligence tests
    b. achievement tests
    c. personality tests
    d. aptitude tests

7. Recent research has confirmed that personality tests
    a. are totally unrelated to most jobs.
    b. can help companies hire more effective workers.
    c. should only be used for low skill jobs.
    d. can harm applicants who have to take the tests.

8. The type of tests that assess the types of activities in which a person is interested is known as
    a. intelligence tests
    b. aptitude tests
    c. interest inventories
    d. personality inventories

9. Requiring an applicant for a sales job to make a sales presentation for a product sold by the company would be an example of using which selection technique?
    a. intelligence tests
    b. aptitude tests
    c. work sampling
    d. ability tests

10. Which of the following is not a typical exercise used in assessment centers?
    a. work sampling
    b. in-baskets
    c. leaderless group discussion
    d. management games

11. The main reason employers use background investigations and reference checks is to
    a. be able to complete the required EEO form asking if this information was collected.
    b. verify the accuracy of factual information provided by the applicant and discover damaging background information.
    c. have information for making the final selection decision about an applicant.
    d. give the personnel representatives in the human resources department something to do.

12. Tests designed to predict such things as proneness to dishonesty and other forms of counter-productivity are referred to as
    a. personality tests
    b. paper-and-pencil honesty tests
    c. aptitude tests
    d. interest tests

13. When can an employer require that a prospective employee have a physical examination?
    a. only after the person starts work
    b. after the job offer is made and before the person starts work
    c. at anytime during the selection process
    d. you can't require physical exams

14. The most common practice relative to drug testing is to
    a. test job candidates before they are formally hired.
    b. test only job incumbents.
    c. test new employees immediately after they are hired.
    d. not use drug tests unless an accident occurs.

15. The purpose of the Immigration Reform and Control Act is to
    a. require all aliens to register for the draft.
    b. prevent aliens from working in the U. S.
    c. require employees to prove they are eligible to be employed in the U. S.
    d. increase the paperwork requirements of employers.

Essays

1. Discuss why validity is important in the selection process.

2. Describe the steps required to validate a test.

3. Identify three types of selection tests and discuss how they can help an employer obtain the most qualified job applicants.

4. Describe the assessment center process and discuss the value of such a process in the selection of employees.

5. Discuss the issues employers need to consider when conducting background investigations and reference checks.

ANSWER KEY

Match Terms with Definitions

1. j   (p. 172)
2. b   (p. 173)
3. f   (p. 173)
4. a   (p. 176)
5. e   (p. 181)
6. d   (p. 183)
7. h   (p. 183)
8. c   (p. 184)
9. g   (p. 180)
10. i (p. 188)

True/False

1. T   (p. 171)
2. F   (p. 171)
3. F   (p. 172-173)
4. T   (p. 173)
5. T   (p. 178)
6. F   (p. 180-181)
7. T   (p. 183)
8. F   (p. 185)
9. F   (p. 188)
10. T (p. 195)
11. T (p. 199)
12. F (p. 201)

Multiple Choice

1. c   (p. 173)
2. c   (p. 173)
3. b   (p. 175)
4. a   (p. 178)
5. d   (p. 178)
6. a   (p. 180-181)
7. b   (p. 183)
8. c   (p. 183-184)
9. c   (p. 185)
10. a (p. 185-186)
11. b (p. 188)
12. b (p. 195-197)
13. b (p. 199)
14. a (p. 199)
15. c (p. 201)

Essay

1. Pages 172-173
2. Pages 174-176
3. Pages 180-184
4. Pages 185-186
5. Pages 188-194

CHAPTER 6

INTERVIEWING CANDIDATES

CHAPTER DESCRIPTION

This chapter describes the various types of interviews used by managers as well as the factors that can undermine the usefulness of the interview. Additionally, the chapter describes the process to use to ensure that interviews are job-related and fairly conducted.

CHAPTER OBJECTIVES

1. Describe several basic types of interviews.
2. Explain the factors and problems that can undermine an interview's usefulness and techniques for eliminating them.
3. List important "guidelines for interviewers."
4. Explain how to develop a structured or situational interview.
5. Discuss how to improve your performance as an interviewer.

CHAPTER STUDY OUTLINE

I. Basic Features of Interviews
   A. Interview is procedure designed to obtain information from person's oral responses to oral inquiries
   B. Selection interview is selection procedure for predicting future job performance based on applicants' oral responses to oral inquiries
   C. Types of interviews
      1. Structured vs. unstructured interviews
         a. Unstructured (nondirective)
         b. Structured (directive)
      2. Classification of interviews by purpose
         a. Stress interview
         b. Appraisal interview
      3. Classification of interviews by content
         a. Situational type of interview
         b. Job-related interviews
      4. Classification of interview based on administration
         a. Structured sequential
         b. Panel interview
         c. Psychological interviews
         d. Computerized selection interview
   D. How useful are interviews?
      1. Research shows usefulness
      2. Important for interviews to be structured
   E. Interviewing and the law: Employment discrimination "testers"
      1. Must adhere to EEOC guidelines
      2. Testers – individuals who apply for employment they don't intend to accept solely to uncover unlawful practices

II. What Factors can Undermine an Interview's Usefulness?
   A. Snap judgments
   B. Negative emphasis
   C. Misunderstanding the job
   D. Pressure to hire

E. Candidate-order (contrast) error
   F. Influence of nonverbal behavior
   G. Telegraphing
   H. Too much/too little talking
   I. Playing district attorney or psychologist

III. Designing and Conducting the Effective Interview
   A. Structured interview
      1. Conduct job analysis
      2. Evaluate job duty information
      3. Develop interview questions
      4. Develop benchmark answers
      5. Appoint interview panel and implement
   B. Guidelines for conducting interview
      1. Structure the interview
         a. Base questions on job analysis
         b. Use objective, specific, behaviorally-oriented questions and criteria
         c. Train interviewers
         d. Use same questions with all candidates
         e. Use rating scales to rate interviewees' answers
         f. Use multiple interviewers or panel interviews
         g. Use better questions (more objective, work related)
      2. Plan the interview
      3. Establish rapport
      4. Ask questions
      5. Close the interview
      6. Review the interview

CHAPTER STUDY QUIZZES

Match Terms with Definitions

a. directive interview
b. situational interview
c. structured sequential interview
d. contrast error
e. snap judgment
f. negative emphasis
g. panel interview
h. stress interview
i. telegraphing
j. playing psychologist

_____ 1. Type of interview in which the questions focus on the individual's ability to project what his or her behavior would be in a given situation.

_____ 2. Type of interview in which questions and acceptable responses are specified in advance and responses are rated for appropriateness of content.

_____ 3. Type of interview in which the candidate is interviewed simultaneously by a group of interviewers.

_____ 4. Type of interview is which the applicant is made uncomfortable by a series of sometimes rude questions.

_____ 5. When an interviewer makes a decision about an applicant within the first few minutes of the interview.

_____ 6. When an interviewer makes a decision about an applicant based on negative information the interviewer has about the applicant.

_____ 7. Type of interview in which interviewer rates candidate on a standard evaluation form and the ratings are compared with those of others, who interviewed the applicant at different times, before a hiring decision is made.

_____ 8. Letting the order in which the interviewer sees applicants affect how the applicants are rated.

_____ 9. When an interviewer focuses on the inconsistencies in the applicant's responses.

_____ 10. When an interviewer helps the applicant respond correctly to questions.

True/False

1. T F Directive interviews involve asking candidates whatever questions come to mind.

2. T F The purpose of the appraisal interview is to select the most qualified applicant for the job.

3. T F A situational interview involves asking questions focusing on the individual's ability to project what his or her behavior would be in a given situation.

4. T F In a panel interview, a candidate is interviewed simultaneously by a group of interviewers.

5. T F Typically, computerized interviews involve only multiple-choice questions.

6. T F An employment tester is someone who does not intend to accept the job if offered.

7. T F Resume data and test scores do not affect an interviewer's initial assessment of a job candidate.

8. T F Contrast error means that the order in which you see applicants affects how you rate them.

9. T F Benchmark answers to interview questions are impossible to set since the interviewer cannot know how applicants will respond to questions.

10. T F Interview questions should be based on job analysis information.

11. T F Multiple interviewers increase the bias in the evaluation of applicants.

12. T F Establishing rapport with the applicant will put the person at ease and increase the amount of information you obtain from him or her.

Multiple Choice

1. Asking the same questions of all candidates and scoring their responses based on a predetermined scoring system is an example of which type of interview?
   a. nondirective
   b. directive
   c. sequential
   d. panel

2. Asking candidates for a supervisor's position how they would respond if a subordinate came into work late three days in a row is an example of which type of interview?
   a. situational
   b. appraisal
   c. stress
   d. nondirective

3. One advantage of a panel interview is that it
   a. means applicants are only interviewed by one person at a time.
   b. reduces the stress of applicants.
   c. elicits deeper and more meaningful responses.
   d. costs less to conduct.

4. Computer-aided interviews are generally used to
   a. make final selection decisions.
   b. reject totally unacceptable candidates.
   c. select applicants who will move on to a face-to-face interview.
   d. both b and c.

5. Regarding the usefulness of selection interviews, research has shown that interviews, especially if structured, are
   a. totally ineffective, especially when compared with other selection methods.
   b. should not be used because they have low reliability.
   c. are comparable with many other selection techniques and do predict performance.
   d. not cost effective when compared with other selection techniques.

6. One technique employers can use to avoid tester claims is to
   a. have applicants execute a statement that they are applying for the job out of a sincere interest in the job and for no other purpose.
   b. never check references of applicants so that testers cannot claim they were singled out.
   c. not tell interviewers that testers may be present.
   d. train interviewers to not record applicant responses.

7. Interviewers are generally more influenced by which type of information about applicants?
   a. favorable
   b. unfavorable
   c. both favorable and unfavorable equally
   d. unbiased

8. If managers are under pressure to hire employees, they are likely to rate applicants
   a. more favorably
   b. more unfavorably
   c. neither favorably nor unfavorably
   d. somewhat more unfavorably

9. Which of the following nonverbal characteristics affect the outcome of interviews?
   a. applicant behaviors
   b. race
   c. gender
   d. all of the above can affect the outcome

10. The following comment was made in a job interview by the interviewer: "This job calls for handling a lot of stress. You can do that, can't you?" This is an example of the interviewer
    a. doing too much talking
    b. playing psychologist
    c. telegraphing
    d. encouraging

11. The first step in creating a successful interview process is
    a. develop interview questions.
    b. conduct a job analysis.
    c. develop benchmark answers.
    d. evaluate job duty information.

12. One of the most important outcomes of training interviewers is
    a. the likelihood that subsequent interviews will be more job related.
    b. that they will let the human resource department handle future interviews.
    c. the increased opportunity to have interviewers interact with human resource staff.
    d. the likelihood that subsequent interviews will be less job related.

13. A good way to reduce bias in the interview process is to
    a. use different interviewers with every applicant.
    b. use different questions with every applicant.
    c. use the same questions with every applicant.
    d. use the same interviewers but different questions for every applicant.

14. Using better questions in the context of employment interviews involves using questions that are
    a. more subjective and non-work oriented.
    b. more objective and less work oriented.
    c. more objective and work oriented.
    d. more subjective and work oriented.

15. Interviewers should not make an immediate decision about an applicant during the interview because
    a. they won't have enough information about the applicant at that time.
    b. it is better to keep the applicant in suspense for as long as possible.
    c. the applicant doesn't expect a decision then.
    d. the outcome might be affected by a snap judgment on the part of the interviewer.

Essays

1. Discuss the difference between structured and unstructured interviews. Indicate which type is most effective in the selection process and how it can be planned and conducted.

2. Describe what constitutes a job-related interview.

3. Compare structured sequential interviews with panel interviews.

4. How can a company plan and conduct interviews to ensure that interviewers avoid tester claims?

5. Describe five factors that affect the usefulness of interviews.

ANSWER KEY

Match Terms with Definitions

1. b   (p. 418)
2. a   (p. 414)
3. g   (p. 419)
4. h   (p. 418)
5. e   (p. 422)
6. f   (p. 423)
7. c   (p. 419)
8. d   (p. 424)
9. j   (p. 426)
10. i (p. 426)

True/False

1.	F	(p. 414)	5.	T	(p. 420)	9.	F	(p. 427)
2.	F	(p. 418)	6.	T	(p. 422)	10.	T	(p. 428)
3.	T	(p. 418)	7.	F	(p. 422)	11.	F	(p. 429)
4.	T	(p. 418)	8.	T	(p. 424)	12.	T	(p. 431)

Multiple Choice

1.	b	(p. 414)	6.	a	(p. 422)	11.	b	(p. 427)
2.	a	(p. 418)	7.	b	(p. 423)	12.	a	(p. 428)
3.	c	(p. 419)	8.	a	(p. 423)	13.	c	(p. 429)
4.	d	(p. 420)	9.	d	(p. 424-426)	14.	c	(p. 429)
5.	c	(p. 421)	10.	c	(p. 426)	15.	d	(p. 431)

Essay

1. Pages 414-418 & 427-432
2. Pages 418-419
3. Pages 419-420
4. Pages 422
5. Pages 422-426

CHAPTER 7

TRAINING AND DEVELOPING EMPLOYEES

CHAPTER DESCRIPTION

This chapter discusses how to design a successful training program, provides an overview of the various types of training that takes place in organizations, and highlights the importance of understanding the learning process as well as evaluating the training effort.

CHAPTER OBJECTIVES

1. Describe the basic training process.
2. Explain the nature of at least five training techniques.
3. Discuss what management development is and why it is important.
4. Describe the five on- and off-the-job development techniques.
5. Explain why training evaluation is important and how it is best accomplished.

CHAPTER STUDY OUTLINE

I. Orienting Employees
   A. Employee orientation provides new employees with basic information to perform jobs
   B. Socialization is ongoing process of instilling in all employees prevailing attitudes, standards, and values of company

II. The Training Process
   A. Training refers to methods used to give new or present employees skills needed to perform their jobs
   B. Five-step training and development process
      1. Needs analysis
      2. Instructional design
      3. Validation
      4. Implementation
      5. Evaluation and follow-up
   C. Training and learning
      1. Need to understand how people learn
      2. Need to make sure new skills and behaviors from training transfer to job
      3. Need to motivate trainee
      4. Need to provide adequate pretraining preparation
   D. Legal aspects of training
      1. Avoid adverse impact charges
      2. Avoid negligent training charges
   E. Training needs analysis
      1. Task analysis – analysis of job's requirements
      2. Performance analysis – analysis of performance of current employees

III. Training Techniques
   A. On-the-job training (OJT)
      1. Types of OJT
         a. Coaching or understudy method
         b. Observation
         c. Position of assistant
         d. Job rotation

2. Advantages of OJT
     a. Relatively inexpensive
     b. Trainees learn while producing
     c. No need for expensive off-job facilities
  3. Factors for trainers to keep in mind
     a. Preparation of the learner
     b. Presentation of the operation
     c. Performance tryout
     d. Follow-up
  B. Apprenticeship training
  C. Informal learning
  D. Job instruction training (JIT)
  E. Lectures
  F. Programmed learning
  G. Audiovisual techniques
     1. Teletraining
     2. Videoconference distance learning
  H. Vestibule or simulated training
  I. Computer-based training
  J. Training via CD-ROM and the Internet
  K. HR research provides guidelines for effective use of technology

IV. Training for Special Purposes
  A. Literacy training techniques
  B. AIDS education
  C. Diversity training
  D. Customer service training
  E. Training for teamwork and empowerment
  F. Providing employees with lifelong learning

V. Managerial Development and Training Techniques
  A. Management development—any attempt to improve managerial performance by imparting knowledge, changing attitudes, or increasing skills
  B. Managerial on-the-job training
     1. Job rotation
     2. Coaching/understudy approach
     3. Action learning
     4. Case study method
  C. Managerial off-the-job training and development techniques
     1. Management games
     2. Outside seminars
     3. University-related programs
     4. Role playing
     5. Behavior modeling
        a. Modeling
        b. Role playing
        c. Social reinforcement
        d. Transfer of training
     6. In-house development centers
     7. Executive development in global companies

VI. Evaluating the Training Effort
  A. Controlled experimentation
  B. Training effects to measure

1. Reaction
2. Learning
3. Behavior
4. Results

CHAPTER STUDY QUIZZES

Match Terms with Definitions

a. programmed learning
b. vestibule training
c. training
d. job rotation
e. task analysis

f. on-the-job training
g. diversity training
h. employee orientation
i. action learning
j. job instruction training

_____ 1. Process of providing employees with basic background information they need to perform their jobs.

_____ 2. Methods used to give new or present employees skills they need to perform their jobs.

_____ 3. Analysis used to determine the training needs of employees who are new to their jobs.

_____ 4. Having a person learn a job by actually performing it.

_____ 5. Learning a job through a logical sequence of steps.

_____ 6. Presenting questions, facts, or problems to the learner; allowing the person to respond; and providing feedback on the accuracy of his or her answers.

_____ 7. Technique in which trainees learn on the actual or simulated equipment they will use on the job but are actually trained off-the-job.

_____ 8. Training that creates better cross-cultural sensitivity among supervisors and nonsupervisors with the aim of creating more harmonious working relationships among a firm's employees.

_____ 9. Moving management trainees from department to department to broaden their knowledge of all parts of the business.

_____ 10. Giving managers and other employees released time to work full-time on projects, analyzing and solving problems in departments other than their own.

True/False

1. T F Socialization is the ongoing process of instilling in all employees the prevailing attitudes, standards, values, and patterns of behavior expected by the organization.

2. T F The first step in the training and development process is validating the training before an audience.

3. T F To help ensure that trainees understand and remember material that is meaningful, the trainer should start with an overview of the material to be presented.

4. T F Negligent training occurs when an employer trains employees but they don't learn what they are supposed to learn.

5. T F Apprenticeship training involves both classroom and on-the-job training.

6. T F Vestibule or simulation training is conducted on the job.

7. T F According to HR research, one way to ensure the effectiveness of technology-based distance learning is to provide an adequate technical support staff.

8. T F Management development focuses exclusively on the technical aspects of a manager's job.

9. T F Behavior modeling can be used to train first-line supervisors how to handle common supervisor-employee interactions better.

10. T F Careful selection of employees for international assignments is necessary for executive development to be effective.

11. T F The best method for evaluating training effectiveness is trainee reaction to the program.

12. T F Evaluation of learning involves assessing whether trainees acquired the principles, skills, and facts they were supposed to learn.

Multiple Choice

1. Providing information to new employees about the company rules takes place during
    a. employee socialization.
    b. employee orientation.
    c. technical training.
    d. mentoring.

2. Which of the following is not a part of the needs analysis step in the training and development process?
    a. identify specific job performance skills needed to improve performance and productivity
    b. analyze the audience to ensure that the program will be suited to their specific levels of education, experience, and attitudes.
    c. introduce and validate the training before a representative audience
    d. use research to develop specific measurable knowledge and performance objectives

3. Trainees can be motivated by doing all but which of the following?
    a. Having the opportunity for realistic practice.
    b. Receiving immediate feedback on responses.
    c. Using limited visual aids so as not to confuse the trainees.
    d. Letting trainees pace themselves.

4. Verifying that an employee has a significant performance deficiency and determining whether that deficiency should be rectified through training or through some other means involves
    a. task analysis.
    b. learning assessment.
    c. reaction assessment.
    d. performance analysis.

5. The most popular form of on-the-job training involves coaching or the understudy method. This means that the employee is trained by whom?
    a. someone from human resources
    b. someone from outside of the organization
    c. a computer-assisted learning program
    d. an experienced worker or the trainee's supervisor

6. Having a master craftsman provide the training occurs as part of
   a. apprenticeship training.
   b. job instruction training.
   c. informal learning.
   d. programmed learning.

7. Successful lectures as a form of training require that the lecturer do all but which of the following?
   a. give your listeners signals to help them follow your ideas
   b. keep your conclusions short
   c. practice
   d. talk from a script rather than from notes

8. A trainer in one location providing training to employees at multiple locations via television hookup is an example of
   a. videoconference distance learning.
   b. apprenticeship training.
   c. programmed instruction.
   d. teletraining.

9. Training designed to teach problem-solving and analysis skills, such as basic statistical analysis and accounting, is designed to
   a. empower employees.
   b. provide better customer service.
   c. address illiteracy.
   d. serve as management development.

10. Presenting an employee with a written description of an organizational problem and having him or her conduct an analysis, diagnose the problem, and present findings is an example of using which management development technique?
    a. action learning
    b. case study method
    c. coaching/understudy approach
    d. in-basket approach

11. Which of the following is not part of the basic behavior modeling procedure?
    a. modeling
    b. job rotation
    c. social reinforcement
    d. transfer of training

12. To reduce the likelihood of failure of employees on overseas assignments, the company should
    a. consider personality and family situations when making assignments.
    b. let employees figure out for themselves how to adapt to the new culture.
    c. only send people who have never been abroad.
    d. don't worry about the repatriation process.

13. Evaluating a training program by assessing and comparing the quality of production of a group that received training on quality and a group that didn't receive the training provides an example of
    a. reaction assessment.
    b. learning assessment.
    c. manipulated experimentation.
    d. controlled experimentation.

14. Asking participants in a training program to indicate how they felt about the training is an example of which type of training outcomes assessment?
    a. reaction
    b. learning
    c. behavior
    d. results

15. Assessing what are the true outcomes for the organization of the training is an example of which type of training outcomes assessment?
    a. reaction
    b. learning
    c. behavior
    d. results

Essays

1. Discuss the five steps in the training and development process and why each is important to include.

2. What should trainers keep in mind if they want to make it easier for trainees to understand and remember material that is taught?

3. Briefly describe the precautions employers should follow to prevent legal problems relative to training programs.

4. Discuss the concept of management development, giving examples of the types of training that can be used for management development.

5. Describe the four basic categories of assessing learning outcomes.

ANSWER KEY

Match Terms with Definitions

1. h (p. 447)
2. c (p. 447)
3. e (p. 453)
4. f (p. 455)
5. j (p. 457-458)
6. a (p. 459)
7. b (p. 461)
8. g (p. 467-468)
9. d (p. 470-471)
10. i (p. 471)

True/False

1. T (p. 447)
2. F (p. 449)
3. T (p. 451)
4. F (p. 452)
5. T (p. 457)
6. F (p. 461)
7. T (p. 463)
8. F (p. 469-470)
9. T (p. 476)
10. T (p. 477)
11. F (p. 479)
12. T (p. 480)

Multiple Choice

1. b (p. 447)
2. c (p. 449)
3. c (p. 451)
4. d (p. 453)
5. d (p. 456)
6. a (p. 457)
7. d (p. 458-459)
8. d (p. 460)
9. a (p. 468-469)
10. b (p. 471)
11. b (p. 476)
12. a (p. 477-478)
13. d (p. 479)
14. a (p. 480)
15. d (p. 480)

Essay

1. Pages 449-450
2. Pages 451
3. Pages 452
4. Pages 469-478
5. Pages 480

CHAPTER 8

MANAGING ORGANIZATIONAL RENEWAL

CHAPTER DESCRIPTION

This chapter provides an introduction to the organizational change process, discusses how to manage organizational change and total quality management programs, and emphasizes the importance of human resources in ensuring that change is effective.

CHAPTER OBJECTIVES

1. Discuss how to manage an organizational change program.
2. Explain how to set up and manage total quality management programs.
3. Describe how to create effective self-directed teams.
4. Discuss HR's role in business process reengineering.

CHAPTER STUDY OUTLINE

I. Managing Organizational Change and Development
   A. What to change?
      1. Strategic change – change in firm's strategy, mission, and vision
      2. Cultural change – change in firm's shared values and aims
         a. Make it clear to employees what you pay attention to, measure, and control
         b. React appropriately to critical incidents and organizational crises
         c. Deliberately role model, teach, and coach the values you want to emphasize
         d. Communicate your priorities by the way you allocate rewards and status
         e. Make your HR procedures and criteria consistent with values you espouse
      3. Structural change – reorganizing and redesigning the organization's departmentalization, coordination, span of control, reporting relationships, or centralization of decision making
      4. Task redesign –changing tasks and authority assigned to individuals
      5. Technological change—modifications to work methods used to accomplish tasks
      6. Changes in people, attitudes, and skills
   B. Ten-step process of leading organizational change
      1. Lewin's process
         a. Unfreezing
         b. Moving
         c. Refreezing
      2. Recent conceptualization of change process
         a. Establish sense of urgency
         b. Mobilize commitment to change through joint diagnosis of business problems
         c. Create a guiding coalition
         d. Develop a shared vision
         e. Communicate the vision
         f. Enable employees to facilitate the change
         g. Generate short-term wins
         h. Consolidate gains and produce more change
         i. Anchor the new ways of doing things in the company's culture
         j. Monitor progress and adjust vision as required
      3. Example
         a. Visioning
         b. Organizational design event
         c. Implementation event

C. Using organizational development to change organizations
   1. Organizational development (OD)
      a. Special approach to organizational change in which employees formulate change that is required and implement it, often with assistance of consultant
      b. Based on specific characteristics
         (1) Action research as basis
         (2) Applies behavioral science knowledge to improve organizational effectiveness
         (3) Changes attitudes, values, and beliefs of employees
         (4) Changes organization in a particular direction
   2. Types of OD applications
      a. Human process applications
         (1) Sensitivity training
         (2) T-groups
      b. Team building
         (1) Confrontation meetings
         (2) Survey research
      c. Technostructural interventions
      d. Human resource management applications
      e. Strategic applications – integrated strategic management

II. Instituting Total Quality Management Programs
   A. What is quality?
      1. Totality of features and characteristics of a product or service that bears on its ability to satisfy given needs
      2. ISO 9000 – quality standards of European community
   B. Total quality management programs
      1. Total quality management (TQM)—continuous improvement, zero defects, six sigma
      2. Malcolm Baldridge Award
   C. TQM at Florida Power and Light (FPL)
      1. Policy deployment
      2. Quality improvement teams
         a. Functional teams
         b. Cross-functional teams
         c. Lead teams
      3. Quality in daily work
   D. Human resource management and the quality improvement effort
      1. Lessons from FPL
      2. HR's role in winning Baldridge Award
      3. HR and ISO 9000

III. Creating Team-Based Organizations
   A. The nature of self-directed teams and worker empowerment
   B. How HR helps to build productive teams
      1. Establish urgent, demanding performance standards
      2. Select members for skill potential
      3. Have team leaders "coach" not "boss"
      4. Challenge group regularly with fresh facts and information
      5. Exploit power of positive feedback, recognition, and reward
      6. Choose people who like teamwork
      7. Train, train, train
      8. Cross-train for flexibility

IV. HR and Business Process Reengineering
   A. What is business process reengineering?
      1. Process reengineering
      2. Fundamentally rethinking business processes to achieve dramatic improvements

- B. HR's role in reengineering processes
  1. Building commitment to reengineering
  2. HR and team building
  3. HR's role in changing the nature of the work
  4. HR's role in moving from controlled to empowered jobs
  5. HR's role in moving from training to education

V. Instituting Flexible Work Arrangements
- A. Flextime
  1. In practice
  2. Pros and cons
  3. Conditions for success
     a. Ensure management support
     b. Make sure is appropriate for the job
     c. Allow flexibility
     d. Install program thoughtfully
- B. Three- and Four-Day Workweeks
  1. Advantages
     a. Increased productivity
     b. Perceived favorably by employees
  2. Disadvantages
     a. Tardiness may become a problem
     b. Fatigue likely to be a problem
- C. Other flexible work arrangements
  1. Job sharing
  2. Work sharing
  3. Flexiplace
  4. Telecommuting
  5. Flexyears

CHAPTER STUDY QUIZZES

Match Terms with Definitions

a. cultural change
b. total quality management
c. ISO 9000
d. self-directed teams
e. sensitivity training
f. flexplace
g. strategic change
h. formal structure technostructural intervention
i. cross-functional teams
j. organizational development

_____ 1. A change in the firm's mission and vision.

_____ 2. A change in the firm's shared values and aims.

_____ 3. An approach to organizational change in which employees themselves formulate change and implement it, often with the assistance of a trained consultant.

_____ 4. Type of training designed to increase participant's insight into his or her own behavior and the behavior of others by encouraging an open expression of feelings.

_____ 5. Change program in which employees collect data on the company's existing organizational structures and then jointly redesign and implement a new one.

_____ 6. Quality standards of the European Community.

_____ 7. Organizationwide programs aimed at maximizing customer satisfaction through continuous improvement.

_____ 8. Ongoing teams formed to address problems that cut across organizational boundaries.

_____ 9. Teams that use consensus decision making to perform tasks such as choosing team members and solving job-related problems.

_____ 10. Program in which employees are allowed to work at home or in a satellite office closer to home.

True/False

1. T F Strategic change involves changing the firm's shared values and aims.

2. T F Establishing a sense of urgency relative to the need for change is necessary to motivate employees to change.

3. T F The purpose of a guiding coalition is solely to write a new mission statement for the company.

4. T F Organizational development is often based on archival research.

5. T F Sensitivity training was one of the earliest OD techniques.

6. T F Survey research provides information that can be fed back to work groups as a basis for problem analysis and action planning.

7. T F ISO 9000 refers to a set of quality standards that customers require vendors to meet.

8. T F Policy deployment is the process through which a company focuses its resources on internal customer satisfaction.

9. T F Organizational human resource development and management is assessed as part of the Malcolm Baldridge application.

10. T F Self-directed teams use consensus decision making to choose their own team members, solve job-related problems, design their own jobs, and schedule their own break time.

11. T F One advantage of flextime is that it is easy to administer.

12. T F Work sharing refers to allowing two or more people to share a single full-time job.

Multiple Choice

1. Implementing a change in the strategy of the organization also often requires changing the shared values and aims of organizational members. This part of the change process requires
   a. structural change.
   b. cultural change.
   c. task redesign.
   d. reengineering.

2. Creating a group of organizational stakeholders who are influential and who can act as missionaries and implementers with regard to organizational change relates to which step in the process for leading organizational change?
   a. establishing a sense of urgency
   b. developing a shared vision
   c. creating a guiding coalition
   d. enabling employees to facilitate the change

3. Organizational development is a special approach to organizational change which applies
   a. scientific knowledge such as that used by chemists and biologists.
   b. economic knowledge such as that used by political leaders.
   c. analytical knowledge such as that used by accountants and engineers.
   d. behavioral science knowledge such as that used by psychologists and other social scientists.

4. The OD activity that can help clarify and bring into the open intergroup misconceptions and problems so that they can be resolved is known as
   a. sensitivity training meetings.
   b. t-group meetings.
   c. confrontation meetings.
   d. team building meetings.

5. Which of the following is not a step in the organizational development intervention of integrated strategic management?
   a. remove all current strategies
   b. analyze current strategy and organizational design
   c. design a strategic change plan
   d. implement a strategic change plan

6. Which of the following is a major reason that has led companies to focus more on quality management?
   a. globalization of competition
   b. simple awareness by management of the need to change
   c. price increases
   d. government regulation

7. The award developed by the U. S. Department of Commerce to recognize quality efforts is the
   a. Henry Kissinger Award
   b. Malcolm Baldridge Award
   c. John F. Kennedy Award
   d. Dwight Eisenhower Award

8. Annual surveys of customer needs led Florida Power and Light to look at the process through which the company focused its resources on achieving customer satisfaction. This process is known as
   a. reengineering.
   b. continuous empowerment.
   c. policy deployment.
   d. implementation.

9. Quality improvement teams that serve as steering committees for all teams that operate in their area are referred to as
   a. functional teams.
   b. cross-functional teams.
   c. lead teams.
   d. self-directed teams.

10. Recognizing that the traditional way of organizing departments and processes around very specialized tasks was duplicative, wasteful, and unresponsive to the firm's customers has led companies to engage in
    a. ISO 9000.
    b. policy deployment.
    c. self-directed work teams.
    d. process reengineering.

11. The work arrangement which allows employees to choose their starting and stopping times is known as
    a. flextime.
    b. flexplace.
    c. work sharing.
    d. job sharing.

12. All but which of the following must be considered if a flextime program is going to be successful?
    a. plan the program and then tell managers to implement it
    b. include a lot of flexibility in the program
    c. appoint a director to coordinate the program
    d. ensure that the program is appropriate for the level of employees

13. Mikaela works from a satellite office near her home three days of the week. She is engaged in which type of work arrangement?
    a. satelliting
    b. telecommuting
    c. flexiplace
    d. flextime

14. Jack and Julio share a single full-time job. They are using the work arrangement known as
    a. work sharing.
    b. job sharing.
    c. flexiplace.
    d. flextime.

15. Under this plan, employees can choose the number of hours they want to work each month over the next year.
    a. flextime
    b. flexplace
    c. work sharing
    d. flexyears

Essays

1. Briefly describe the types of change that can take place in organizations, emphasizing why each is important and how they are related.

2. List the steps in the 10-step process for leading organizational change and then summarize what these steps are designed to accomplish.

3. What is organizational development and how is it accomplished in organizations?

4. Why are companies concerned with total quality management issues?

5. What is the role of human resources in relative to total quality management?

ANSWER KEY

Match Terms with Definitions

1. g (p. 490)
2. a (p. 490)
3. j (p. 494)
4. e (p. 495)

6. c (p. 497)
7. b (p. 498)
8. i (p. 499)
9. d (p. 502)

5. h (p. 497)   10. f (p. 512)

True/False

1. F (p. 490)   5. T (p. 496)   9. T (p. 500)
2. T (p. 492)   6. T (p. 496)   10. T (p. 502)
3. F (p. 492)   7. T (p. 497)   11. F (p. 509)
4. F (p. 494)   8. F (p. 498)   12. F (p. 510)

Multiple Choice

1. b (p. 490)   6. a (p. 497)   11. a (p. 509)
2. c (p. 492)   7. b (p. 498)   12. a (p. 509)
3. d (p. 494)   8. c (p. 498)   13. c (p. 510)
4. c (p. 496)   9. c (p. 499)   14. b (p. 510)
5. a (p. 497)   10. d (p. 507)   15. d (p. 511)

Essay

1. Pages 490-491
2. Pages 491-493
3. Pages 494-497
4. Pages 498-499
5. Pages 499-508

CHAPTER 9

APPRAISING PERFORMANCE

CHAPTER DESCRIPTION

This chapter discusses the various methods used for performance appraisals in organizations, how to conduct effective appraisals, and legal and ethical issues surrounding performance appraisal.

CHAPTER OBJECTIVES

1. Explain why it is important to effectively appraise performance.
2. Describe eight performance appraisal methods and the pros and cons of each.
3. Discuss the major problems inhibiting effective performance appraisals.
4. Conduct a more effective appraisal interview.

CHAPTER STUDY OUTLINE

I. The Appraisal Process
   A. Definition of appraisal
      1. Setting work standards
      2. Assessing employee's actual performance relative to standards
      3. Providing feedback to employee with aim of motivating employee to eliminate performance deficiencies or to continue to perform above par
   B. The supervisor's role in appraisal
      1. HR sets policy and advises on process
      2. Supervisor responsible for conducting appraisal
   C. Steps in appraising performance
      1. Defining the job
      2. Appraising performance
      3. Feedback sessions
   D. Problems with appraisals
      1. Subordinates not told what is expected of them in terms of good performance
      2. Problems with forms or procedures used to appraise performance
      3. Problems with how interview-feedback session conducted
   E. How to clarify expected performance
      1. Set measurable standards
      2. Tell employees ahead of time what the standards are

II. Appraisal Methods
   A. Graphic rating scale method
      1. Simplest and most popular
      2. Lists traits or duties and range of performance values for each trait or duty
   B. Alternation ranking method
      1. List all subordinates
      2. Cross off names of any not known well enough to rank
      3. Indicate employee highest on characteristic being measured, then employee who is lowest, then next highest, next lowest, etc.
   C. Paired comparison method
      1. Each subordinate paired and compared to every other subordinate
      2. Add up number of times an employee is rated better

- D. Forced distribution method
    1. Similar to grading on a curve
    2. Predetermined percentages of ratees placed in performance categories
- E. Critical incident method
    1. Supervisor keeps log of desirable or undesirable examples or incidents of each subordinate's work-related behavior
    2. Every six months or so, supervisor and subordinate meet and discuss subordinate's performance using specific incidents as examples
- F. Narrative forms
    1. Supervisor rates employees' performance in terms of standards
    2. Supervisor presents critical examples and improvement plan
- G. Behaviorally anchored rating scales (BARS)
    1. Process for developing
        a. Generate critical incidents
        b. Develop performance dimensions
        c. Reallocate incidents
        d. Scale the incidents
        e. Develop final instrument
    2. Advantages
        a. More accurate gauge
        b. Clearer standards
        c. Feedback
        d. Independent dimensions
        e. Consistency
- H. Management by Objectives (MBO) Method
    1. Manager sets specific measurable goals with each employee
    2. Manager and employee periodically discuss progress toward goals
    3. Specific steps
        a. Set organization's goals
        b. Set departmental goals
        c. Discuss departmental goals
        d. Define expected results
        e. Performance reviews: Measure the results
        f. Provide feedback
    4. Problems to avoid
        a. Setting unclear unmeasurable objectives
        b. Process is time-consuming
        c. Setting objectives with subordinate sometimes turns into tug of war
- I. Mixing the methods

III. Appraising Performance: Problems and Solutions
- A. Dealing with rating scale appraisal problems
    1. Unclear standards
    2. Halo effect
    3. Central tendency
    4. Leniency or strictness
    5. Bias
- B. How to avoid appraisal problems
    1. Understand problems that can occur
    2. Choose right appraisal tool
    3. Train supervisors to eliminate rating errors
    4. Keep performance diaries

C. Legal and ethical issues in performance appraisal
   1. Subjectivity and inadequate standardization led to EEO problems
   2. Ethics should be bedrock of performance appraisals
   3. To be legally defensible
      a. Conduct job analysis to determine criteria and standards required for successful performance
      b. Incorporate criteria and standards into rating instrument
      c. Use clearly defined individual dimensions of job performance
      d. Communicate performance standards to employees and raters
      e. Avoid abstract trait names on graphic rating scales
      f. Subjective supervisory ratings should be only one part of process
      g. Train supervisors
      h. Allow appraisers substantial daily contact with employees they evaluate
      i. Base appraisals on multiple dimensions
      j. Use multiple appraisers if possible
      k. Don't let one appraiser have absolute authority to determine a personnel action
      l. Include an appeals process
      m. Document all relevant information
      n. Provide corrective guidance for poor performers
D. Who should do the appraising?
   1. Appraisal by immediate supervisor
   2. Peer appraisals
   3. Rating committees
   4. Self-ratings
   5. Appraisal by subordinates
   6. 360-degree feedback

IV. The Appraisal Interview
   A. Types of interviews
      1. Appraisal interview
      2. Satisfactory–promotable
      3. Satisfactory–not promotable
      4. Unsatisfactory–correctable
   B. How to prepare for appraisal interview
      1. Assemble data
      2. Prepare employee
      3. Choose time and place
   C. How to conduct interview
      1. Be direct and specific
      2. Don't get personal
      3. Encourage the person to talk
      4. Don't tiptoe around
   D. How to handle a defensive subordinate
      1. Recognize defensive behavior is normal
      2. Never attack a person's defenses
      3. Postpone action
      4. Recognize your own limitations
   E. How to criticize a subordinate
   F. How to ensure that the appraisal interview leads to improved performance
   G. How to handle a formal written warning

V. Performance Appraisal in Practice

VI. The Role of Appraisals in Managing Performance
   A. Do appraisals really help to improve performance?
   B. TQM-based appraisals for managing performance

CHAPTER STUDY QUIZZES

Match Terms with Definitions

a. critical incident method
b. graphic rating scale
c. leniency problem
d. 360-degree feedback
e. paired comparison method
f. narrative forms
g. central tendency problem
h. alternation ranking method
i. forced distribution method
j. behaviorally-anchored rating scale

_____ 1. An appraisal method in which traits or duties are listed and a range of performance values are included for each trait or duty.

_____ 2. An appraisal method in which employees are ranked alternately from best to worst.

_____ 3. An appraisal method in which every subordinate is paired with and compared to every other subordinate.

_____ 4. An appraisal method in which predetermined percentages of ratees are placed in performance categories.

_____ 5. An appraisal method in which the supervisor keeps a log of desirable or undesirable examples or incidents or each subordinate's work-related behaviors.

_____ 6. An appraisal method in which the supervisor rates the employee's performance in terms of standards and presents critical examples and an improvement plan.

_____ 7. An appraisal method that uses critical incidents and quantified ratings.

_____ 8. Rating all employees average on their appraisals.

_____ 9. Rating all employees high on their appraisals.

_____ 10. An appraisal method in which performance information is collected from supervisors, peers, and internal and external customers.

True/False

1. T F The human resource department has complete responsibility for conducting performance appraisals.

2. T F Appraisals are used for making promotion and salary decisions.

3. T F Effective performance appraisals begin with defining the job and its standards.

4. T F The behaviorally anchored scale is the simplest and most popular technique for appraising performance.

5. T F The alternation ranking method of appraisal involves rating employees from best to worse.

6. T F The forced distribution method of performance appraisal is similar to grading on a curve.

7. T F The critical incident method of appraisal focuses only on poor performance.

8. T F When using management by objectives, the supervisor sets the goals for the employee.

9. T F The halo effect occurs when the rating of a subordinate on one major trait biases the way you rate that person on other traits.

10. T F Rater training will solve all problems with performance appraisals.

11. T F Courts have found that inadequacies in employer appraisal systems are at the root of illegal discriminatory actions.

12. T F In 360-degree feedback, the employee's supervisor is the only person who provides feedback about the employee's performance.

Multiple Choice

1. In the context of the performance appraisal process, "defining the job" means
   a. conducting a job analysis.
   b. making sure that you and your subordinate agree on his or her job duties and job standards.
   c. telling your employee what his or her job standards are going to be.
   d. writing a new job description right before you conduct the appraisal.

2. Which of the following is a good example of how to set measurable standards when operationalizing performance expectations for the job of sales manager?
   a. Keep the sales force happy by giving them incentives.
   b. Increase sales in your region.
   c. Increase sales in your region by 15% by the end of the next quarter.
   d. Keep customers away from executives.

3. In evaluating your subordinates, you rank Jaime as best in terms of overall performance, Paul as worst, Janice as next best, Jill as next worst, and so on. You are using which method of performance appraisal?
   a. graphic rating scale
   b. alternation ranking
   c. forced distribution
   d. paired comparison

4. Only 25% of your employees can be rated as above average and 25% must be rated as below average. All other employees are rated average. You are being required to use which method of performance appraisal?
   a. graphic rating scale
   b. alternation ranking
   c. forced distribution
   d. paired comparison

5. This method of performance appraisal involves identifying critical incidents of effective and ineffective performance and using that information to develop anchors for the scale used for each performance dimension being evaluated.
   a. graphic rating scale
   b. forced distribution
   c. critical incident
   d. behaviorally-anchored rating scale

6. Which of the following is not a problem when using management by objectives (MBO)?
   a. deciding who should provide the 360-degree feedback
   b. setting unclear, unmeasurable objectives
   c. not recognizing that MBO is time consuming
   d. not knowing enough about the person and the job

7. Tianna rated all of her subordinates as below average on their performance appraisals. She said that this was a good way to motivate performance. She is guilty of which performance appraisal problem?
   a. bias
   b. central tendency
   c. strictness
   d. leniency

8. Allowing ratee characteristics such as age, race, and gender to affect their performance appraisal ratings is an example of which type of rating problem?
   a. bias
   b. central tendency
   c. strictness
   d. leniency

9. Juanita was always friendly to customers. Her supervisor, consequently, rated Juanita high on all dimensions of the performance appraisal even though Juanita often came to work late, did not finish tasks on time, and was the only member of the department who would not assist coworkers. This is an example of which rating problem?
   a. bias
   b. strictness
   c. central tendency
   d. halo effect

10. All but which of the following are recommendations for minimizing the impact of performance appraisals such as bias and central tendency?
    a. only do performance appraisals once a year
    b. choose the right appraisal tool
    c. train supervisors to avoid rating errors
    d. keep performance diaries

11. When subordinates anonymously evaluate their supervisors' performance, the process is referred to as
    a. downward feedback
    b. 360-degree appraisal
    c. upward feedback
    d. vertical feedback

12. Which of the following is not a step in preparing for the appraisal interview?
    a. assemble the data
    b. prepare the employee
    c. choose the time and place
    d. invite the employee's subordinates

13. The best way to provide constructive feedback to an employee is to
    a. just lay the problems on the line and tell the person to improve.
    b. provide examples of critical incidents and specific suggestions of what could be done and why.
    c. just give the employee his or her evaluation form to read.
    d. make the feedback personal so that the employee will understand that he or she is a problem.

14. Which of the following is a specific purpose for using formal written warnings about an employee's poor performance?
    a. They may serve to shake your employee out of his or her bad habits.
    b. They cannot help you defend your rating of the employee to either your boss or the courts but are good to do anyway.
    c. They make the supervisor feel that at least he or she has done something.
    d. They provide the employee ammunition to use in court about the supervisor's poor judgment.

15. The best way to describe the aim of performance management in TQM-oriented companies is
    a. to provide the supervisors with greater guidance for evaluating employees.
    b. to establish systems that encourage employees to become committed partners in the tasks of boosting quality and performance.
    c. to establish guidelines for exactly what the employee is supposed to do on the job.
    d. to provide a subjective means for evaluating employee performance.

Essays

1. Discuss the reasons that performance appraisal is important.

2. Compare and contrast five types of performance appraisal methods.

3. What are some of the problems associated with performance appraisals?

4. What legal issues does a supervisor need to be aware of when conducting performance appraisals?

5. Describe what needs to be done to conduct an effective performance appraisal interview.

ANSWER KEY

Match Terms with Definitions

1. b   (p. 321)
2. h   (p. 323)
3. e   (p. 325)
4. i   (p. 325)
5. a   (p. 327)
6. f   (p. 329)
7. j   (p. 329-330)
8. g   (p. 336)
9. c   (p. 336)
10. d (p. 343)

True/False

1. F   (p. 320)
2. T   (p. 320)
3. T   (p. 321)
4. F   (p. 321)
5. T   (p. 323)
6. T   (p. 325)
7. F   (p. 327)
8. F   (p. 331)
9. T   (p. 336)
10. F (p. 338)
11. T (p. 340)
12. F (p. 343)

Multiple Choice

1. b   (p. 320)
2. c   (p. 321)
3. b   (p. 323)
4. c   (p. 325)
5. d   (p. 329-331)
6. a   (p. 332)
7. c   (p. 336)
8. a   (p. 337)
9. d   (p. 336)
10. a (p. 338)
11. c (p. 342)
12. d (p. 345)
13. b (p. 347)
14. a (p. 347)
15. b (p. 349)

Essay

1. Page 320
2. Pages 321-335
3. Pages 335-339
4. Pages 340-341
5. Pages 345-347

CHAPTER 10

MANAGING CAREERS AND FAIR TREATMENT

CHAPTER DESCRIPTION

This chapter reviews the factors that affect career choices as well as the role of the individual, manager, and employer in career development. Also discussed are guidelines for ensuring fair treatment of employees and managing the discipline process.

CHAPTER OBJECTIVES

1. Discuss the factors that affect career choices.
2. Explain how you would make a new subordinate's first assignment more meaningful.
3. Discuss how to more effectively manage promotions and transfers.
4. Explain in detail techniques for building two-way communications in organizations.
5. Discuss how to discipline employees.
6. Define wrongful discharge and explain its importance.
7. Explain how to dismiss an employee.

CHAPTER STUDY OUTLINE

I. The Basics of Career Management
   A. Roles in career development
      1. Individual
         a. Assess own interests, skills, and values
         b. Take steps to ensure a happy and fulfilling career
      2. Manager
         a. Provide timely and objective performance feedback
         b. Offer developmental assignments and support
         c. Participate in career oriented appraisals
      3. Employer
         a. Provide career-oriented training and development opportunities
         b. Offer career management programs
         c. Establish career-oriented appraisal and job-posting policies
         d. Career-oriented actions
            (1) Avoid reality shock
            (2) Provide challenging initial jobs
            (3) Provide realistic job previews in recruiting
            (4) Be demanding
            (5) Provide periodic job rotation and job pathing
            (6) Do career-oriented performance appraisals
            (7) Provide career planning workshops and career planning workbooks
            (8) Provide mentoring opportunities
   B. Making promotion decisions

II. Managing Promotions and Transfers
   A. Decisions
      1. Decision 1: Is seniority or competence the rule?
      2. Decision 2: How is competence measured?
      3. Decision 3: Is the process formal or informal?
      4. Decision 4: Vertical, horizontal, or other?
   B. Handling transfers

       1. Reasons for transfers
       2. Effect on family life
   C. Career management and commitment
       1. Developmental activities
       2. Career-oriented appraisals
       3. Career records/jobs posting systems

III. Managing Fair Treatment
   A. Introduction: The building blocks of fairness
   B. Build two-way communications
       1. "Speak-up!" programs
       2. What's your opinion?
       3. Top down programs
   C. Emphasize fairness in disciplining—nonpunitive discipline
   D. Manage employee privacy

IV. Managing Dismissals
   A. Dismissal
   B. Terminate at will
   C. Grounds for dismissal
       1. Misconduct
       2. Insubordination
   D. Avoiding wrongful discharge suits
       1. Wrongful discharge—when an employee violates the law or the contractual arrangements stated or implied by the firm
       2. Avoiding wrongful discharge
          a. Institute employment policies and dispute resolution procedures that make employees feel they are treated fairly
          b. Do preparatory work that will help avoid wrongful discharge suits before they get started
   E. The termination interview--plan the interview carefully and get to the point
       1. Outplacement counseling
       2. Exit interview
   F. Layoffs and the plant closing law
       1. The plant closing law
       2. Bumping/layoff procedures
       3. Alternatives to layoffs
   G. Adjusting to downsizings and mergers
       1. Downsizing
       2. Handling the merger/acquisition
   H. Retirement

CHAPTER STUDY QUIZZES

Match Terms with Definitions

a. mentoring
b. outplacement counseling
c. downsizing
d. dismissal
e. insubordination
f. discipline
g. layoff
h. terminate at will
i. reality shock
j. wrongful discharge

_____ 1. May occur at initial career entry when a new employee's high job expectations are not met.

_____ 2. Use of an experienced individual to teach and train someone with less knowledge in a given area.

_____ 3. Activities designed to cause employees to behave sensibly at work (where sensible is defined as adhering to rules and regulations).

_____ 4. Terminating an employee after all reasonable steps to rehabilitate or salvage the employee have failed.

_____ 5. The employee can resign for any reason, at will, and the employer could similarly dismiss an employee for any reason, at will.

_____ 6. A form of misconduct that is sometimes the grounds for dismissal

_____ 7. Occurs when an employee's dismissal violates the law or the contractual arrangements stated or implied by the firm via its employment application forms, manuals, or other promises.

_____ 8. Systematic process by which a terminated person is trained and counseled in the techniques of conducting a self-appraisal and securing a new job that is appropriate to his or her needs and talents.

_____ 9. When workers are sent home for a time because there is no work available, management expects the no-work situation to be temporary and probably short-term, and management intends to recall the employees when work is again available.

_____ 10. Reducing, usually dramatically, the number of people employed by the firm.

True/False

1. T F Only the employee has a role in career development.

2. T F Research has shown that providing challenging first jobs for individuals is a powerful means of aiding career development of new employees.

3. T F Organizational mentoring is a formal process whereby junior employees are assigned to senior employees for purposes of the senior employee coaching the junior employee.

4. T F Promotions should only be based on seniority.

5. T F "Speak-up!" Programs are designed to encourage upward communications within organizations.

6. T F Opinion surveys are anonymous surveys designed to allow employees to express feelings about the company and its managers.

7. T F Rules and regulations serve about the same purpose in organizations that laws do in society.

8. T F The purpose of a paid one-day "decision-making leave" is to reward the employee for staying with the company.

9. T F Dismissal is the most drastic disciplinary step you can take against an employee.

10. T F Direct disregard of one's boss, deliberate defiance of clearly stated company policy, and public criticism of the boss are all examples of insubordination.

11. T F Requiring employees to sign the employment application and making sure it contains a clearly worded statement that the employment is for no fixed term and that the employer can terminate the employee at any time will help avoid wrongful discharge lawsuits.

12. T F Preretirement counseling occurs when an employee accepts a job for the sole purpose of explaining the retirement package.

Multiple Choice

1. The human resource activity of _____ has as its career development focus to add development plans and individual goal setting.
   a. human resource planning
   b. training and development
   c. performance appraisal
   d. recruiting and placement

2. The human resource activity of _____ has as its career development focus to provide career path information and add individual growth orientation.
   a. human resource planning
   b. training and development
   c. performance appraisal
   d. recruiting and placement

3. The role of the manager in career development is to
   a. assess employee skills, interests, and values.
   b. offer career management programs.
   c. establish job-posting policies.
   d. offer developmental assignments.

4. The best way that new employees can test themselves and crystallize their career anchors is to
   a. work in the same job in a number of different companies.
   b. try out a variety of challenging jobs in various specializations.
   c. continue to take college courses.
   d. work in the same job in a number of different departments within the same company.

5. From the point of view of motivation of employees, which of the following is the best criterion to use for making promotion decisions?
   a. competence
   b. seniority
   c. subjective supervisory appraisals
   d. union status

6. Research has shown what about the effect on an employee's family life of having frequent transfers?
   a. There are major differences between mobile and stable families.
   b. Mobile families are better than stable families.
   c. Stable families are better than mobile families.
   d. There are few differences between mobile and stable families.

7. Which of the following statements has research shown to be true about fairness and employee communication?
   a. The "squeaky wheel gets the grease."
   b. Individuals who communicate assertively were more likely to be treated fairly by the decision maker.
   c. Individuals who communicate aggressively were more likely to be treated fairly by the decision maker.
   d. Individuals who communicate passively were more likely to be treated fairly by the decision maker.

8. The purpose of discipline in organizations is to
    a. encourage employees to behave sensibly at work.
    b. crack the whip so employees will do as they are told.
    c. give supervisors a means for getting rid of employees they don't like.
    d. make sure that employees are organized and ready to work.

9. Which of the following is not a basis for dismissing employees?
    a. satisfactory performance
    b. misconduct
    c. lack of qualifications for the job
    d. changed requirements of the job

10. To reduce the likelihood that an employee can win a wrongful discharge suit, the employer should
    a. not allow anyone but representatives from the human resource department to talk to job applicants.
    b. not make any implied or explicit comments to employees about job security.
    c. have a lawyer handle all negotiations with prospective employees.
    d. have as little information as possible in the employee handbook.

11. The purpose of exit interviews is to
    a. give the employee information he or she will need after leaving the company.
    b. tell the employee what he or she is allowed to say about the company in the future.
    c. elicit information about the job or related matters that might give the employer a better insight into what is right—or wrong—about the company.
    d. ensure that the employee will leave the company on a positive note because an interview was held.

12. The Plant Closing Law applies to employers of _____ or more employees and requires that the employers give the employees _____ days notice before closing a facility or starting a layoff of _____ or more people.
    a. 100; 90; 50
    b. 50; 30; 100
    c. 75; 180; 100
    d. 100; 60; 50

13. The most frequently used criterion for making layoff decisions is
    a. seniority.
    b. competence.
    c. age.
    d. gender.

14. Which of the following statements is true about downsizing?
    a. Downsizing has been proven to be an effective cost cutter for all organizations.
    b. Many firms that downsize don't experience the anticipated cost savings because they don't actually eliminate all employees they claim were let go.
    c. Retained employees generally have no problem adjusting after a downsizing.
    d. Downsizing is no longer used as an organizational strategy.

15. The purpose of preretirement counseling is to
    a. ease the passage of employees into retirement.
    b. boost the amount of funds in the company's retirement pool.
    c. encourage employees to take early retirement.
    d. make the company look good.

Essays

1. What can employers do to assist employees with career development?

2. Describe the decisions employers must consider when making promotion decisions.

3. What does it mean for employers to ensure fair treatment of employees and how can this be accomplished?

4. Discuss how employers can discipline without punishment and why this approach is important.

5. Explain the four bases employers have for dismissing employees.

ANSWER KEY

Match Terms with Definitions

1. i   (p. 362)
2. a   (p. 364)
3. f   (p. 373-374)
4. d   (p. 376)
5. h   (p. 376)
6. e   (p. 377)
7. j   (p. 378)
8. b   (p. 381)
9. g   (p. 382)
10. c (p. 383)

True/False

1. F   (p. 361)
2. T   (p. 363)
3. F   (p. 364)
4. F   (p. 364-367)
5. T   (p. 372)
6. T   (p. 373)
7. T   (p. 373)
8. F   (p. 374)
9. T   (p. 376)
10. T (p. 377)
11. T (p. 378)
12. F (p. 384)

Multiple Choice

1. c   (p. 361)
2. b   (p. 361)
3. d   (p. 361-362)
4. b   (p. 363)
5. a   (p. 364)
6. d   (p. 368)
7. b   (p. 372)
8. a   (p. 373)
9. a   (p. 377-378)
10. b (p. 378-380)
11. c (p. 381)
12. d (p. 382)
13. a (p. 382)
14. b (p. 383)
15. a (p. 384)

Essay

1. Pages 362-364
2. Pages 364-367
3. Pages 372-373
4. Pages 374-375
5. Pages 377-378

CHAPTER 11

ESTABLISHING PAY PLANS

CHAPTER DESCRIPTION

This chapter describes the procedures used by organizations to determine pay rates for employees, explains the basic steps involved in establishing specific pay rates, and reviews laws that specifically impact wages.

CHAPTER OBJECTIVES

1. Discuss four basic factors determining pay rates.
2. Explain in detail each of the five basic steps in establishing pay rates.
3. Present the pros and cons of job evaluation.
4. Define comparable worth and explain its importance today.

CHAPTER STUDY OUTLINE

I. Basic Aspects of Compensation
   A. Direct financial payments
      1. Based on increments of time
      2. Pay for performance
   B. Indirect financial payments

II. Basic Considerations in Determining Pay Rates
   A. Legal considerations in compensation
      1. 1931 Davis-Bacon Act
      2. 1936 Walsh-Healey Public Contract Act
      3. 1938 Fair Labor Standards Act
      4. 1963 Equal Pay Act
      5. 1964 Civil Rights Act
      6. 1974 Employee Retirement Income Security Act (ERISA)
      7. The Tax Reform Act of 1986
      8. Other legislation affecting compensation
         a. Age Discrimination in Employment Act (ADEA)
         b. Americans with Disabilities Act
         c. Family and Medical Leave Act
         d. Workers' compensation laws
         e. Social Security Act
         f. Unemployment compensation
         g. Federal wage garnishment law
   B. Union influences on compensation decisions
      1. National Labor Relations Act of 1935 (Wagner Act)
      2. National Labor Relations Board
   C. Compensation policies
   D. Equity and its impact on pay rates

III. Establishing Pay Rates
   A. Step 1. Conduct the salary survey
      1. Salary surveys
         a. Commercial

- b. Professional
- c. Government
- d. Internet
2. Benchmark jobs

B. Step 2. Determine the worth of each job: Job evaluation.
1. Purpose
2. Compensable factors
   a. Determine definition of job content
   b. Establish how jobs compare to each other
   c. Set compensation paid for each job
3. Planning and preparation for the job evaluation
   a. Identify the need for the program
   b. Gain employee cooperation
   c. Choose a job evaluation committee
      (1) Identifies 10 to 15 key benchmark jobs
      (2) Select compensable factors
      (3) Evaluate worth of the jobs
4. Ranking method of job evaluation
   a. Obtain job information
   b. Select raters and jobs to be rated
   c. Select compensable factors
   d. Rank jobs
   e. Pros—simple, easiest to explain, takes less time than other methods
   f. Cons—relies too heavily on guesstimates, provides no yardstick for measuring value of one job relative to another
5. Job classification (or grading) evaluation method
   a. Classes – contain similar jobs
   b. Grades—contain jobs similar in difficulty but otherwise different
   c. Procedure
      (1) Choose compensable factors
      (2) Develop class or grade descriptions that describe each class in terms of amount or level of compensable factors in jobs
   d. Advantages—groups all jobs into classes which employers usually do anyway
   e. Disadvantages—difficult to write class or grade descriptions and considerable judgment required to apply them
6. Point method of job evaluation
   a. More quantitative job evaluation technique
   b. Procedure
      (1) Identify several compensable factors, each having several degrees
      (2) Identify the degree to which each factor is present in the job
7. Factor comparison job evaluation method
   a. Quantitative technique that determines which jobs have more of the chosen compensable factors
   b. Refinement of ranking method
   c. Procedure
      (1) Rank the job on each compensable factor chosen
      (2) Combine rankings into overall numerical rating for the job
   d. Computerized job evaluation

C. Step 3. Group similar jobs into pay grades
D. Step 4. Price each pay grade—wage curves
1. Wage curve depicts graphically pay rates currently being paid for jobs in each pay grade, relative to the points or rankings assigned to each job or grade by the job evaluation
2. Pricing jobs with wage curve

            a. Find average pay for each pay grade
            b. Plot the pay rates for each pay grade
            c. Fit a wage line through the points plotted
            d. Price jobs
    E. Step 5. Fine-tune pay rates
        1. Developing rate ranges
        2. Correcting out-of-line rates (red-circle, flagged, overrates)
            a. Freeze rate paid to employees in this grade until general salary increases bring other jobs into line with it
            b. Transfer or promote some or all of the employees involved to jobs where they can be paid their current rates
            c. Freeze rate for six months, try to promote or transfer employees, then cut pay of remaining employees to maximum for grade

IV. Current Trends in Compensation
    A. Skill-based pay
    B. Broadbanding
    C. Why job evaluation plans are still widely used
    D. The "new" pay

V. Pricing Managerial and Professional Jobs
    A. Compensating managers
        1. Basic compensation elements
        2. Managerial job evaluation
    B. Compensating professional employees

VI. Current Issues in Compensation Management
    A. The issue of comparable worth—requirement to pay equal wages for jobs of comparable value to employer
        1. *Gunther* Supreme Court case
        2. Comparable worth and job evaluation
        3. Implications
    B. The issue of salary compression
    C. The issue of cost-of-living differentials

CHAPTER STUDY QUIZZES

Match Terms with Definitions

a. compensation
b. compensable factors
c. Fair Labor Standards Act
d. Walsh-Healey Public Contract
e. job grade

f. benchmark jobs
g. Davis-Bacon Act
h. Equal Pay Act
i. job evaluation
j. point method

_____ 1. Law that provides for Secretary of Labor to set wage rates for laborers and mechanics employed by contractors working for the federal government.

_____ 2. All forms of pay or rewards going to employees and arising from their employment.

_____ 3. Law that contains minimum wage, maximum hours, overtime pay, equal pay, record-keeping, and child labor provisions covering the majority of U. S. workers.

_____ 4. Law that states that employees of one sex may not be paid wages at a rate lower than that paid to employees of the opposite sex for doing roughly equivalent work.

_____ 5. Law that sets basic labor standards for employees working on any government contract that amounts to more than $10,000.

_____ 6. Jobs that anchor the employer's pay scale and around which other jobs are slotted into the pay scale.

_____ 7. Formal and systematic comparison of jobs to determine the worth of one job relative to another and that eventually results in a wage or survey hierarchy.

_____ 8. Factors that determine your definition of job content, establish how the jobs compare to each other, and set the compensation paid for each job.

_____ 9. A group of jobs that are similar in difficulty but otherwise different.

_____ 10. A quantitative job evaluation technique involving identification of compensable factors and the degree to which each of these factors is present in some job.

True/False

1. T F Employee compensation refers only to wages and salaries.

2. T F The Civil Rights Act of 1964 does not apply to employee compensation issues.

3. T F Each of the 50 states has its own workers' compensation laws which aim to provide prompt, sure, and reasonable income to victims of work-related accidents.

4. T F Salary surveys are formal surveys conducted only by professional organizations.

5. T F Ranking and job classification are both quantitative techniques for conducting job evaluation.

6. T F The main difference between ranking and factor comparison as job evaluation techniques is that the ranking method generally looks at each job as an entity and ranks jobs on some overall factor while factor comparison ranks each job several times—once for each compensable factor chosen.

7. T F A pay grade is comprised of jobs of approximately equal difficulty or importance as determined by job evaluation.

8. T F Skill-based pay involves paying employees based on a prescribed set of compensable factors.

9. T F The four main components of a top executive's pay are base salary, short-term incentives, long-term incentives, and executive benefits and perks.

10. T F The basic trend today in top executive pay is to increase the relative importance of base salary and to reduce the importance of incentives.

11. T F Comparable worth is the same thing as equal pay for equal work.

12. T F Salary compression results from inflation and means that longer-term employees' salaries are lower than those for workers entering the firm today.

Multiple Choice

1. The Fair Labor Standards Act provides that employees covered by the Act who work more than 40 hours per week must be compensated at what rate?
    a. one and a half times the hourly base rate for the person
    b. twice the hourly base rate for the person
    c. two and a half times the hourly base rate for the person
    d. the same as the hourly base rate for the person

2. The Equal Pay Act states that employees of one sex may not be paid wages at a rate lower than that paid to employees of the opposite sex for doing roughly equivalent work. Equal in this case is defined in terms of
    a. knowledge, skills, and abilities.
    b. skills, effort, responsibility, and working conditions.
    c. skill and experience only.
    d. age, experience, and education.

3. Which of the following is not a provision of the Employee Retirement Income Security Act (ERISA)?
    a. regulations regarding vesting rights
    b. portability rights
    c. fiduciary standards to prevent dishonesty
    d. minimum amounts employees can contribute

4. The process of determining a job's relative worth is known as
    a. job analysis.
    b. job comparison.
    c. job evaluation.
    d. job classification.

5. The choice of compensable factors for a job evaluation depend on the method of job evaluation to be used and
    a. the job evaluation committee's preferences.
    b. the nature of the job.
    c. comparable worth information.
    d. benchmark jobs.

6. Which of the following would not be a reason leading to the need for job evaluation?
    a. high turnover
    b. work stoppages
    c. arguments over wage inequities
    d. work duties remaining the same over time

7. A major problem with the ranking method of job evaluation is that
    a. it provides no yardstick for measuring the value of one job relative to another.
    b. the classification descriptions are difficult to write.
    c. there are too many factors to consider.
    d. employees don't understand it.

8. The major difference between the point method of job evaluation and the factor comparison method is that
    a. the point method is a qualitative process while the factor comparison method is a quantitative process.
    b. the point method involves wage curves while the factor comparison method involves job grades.
    c. the point method involves rating jobs relative to the defined compensable factors while the factor comparison method involves ranking each job on each compensable factor.
    d. the point method is a quantitative process while the factor comparison method is a qualitative process.

9. The purpose of the wage curve is to show the relationship between the value of the job as determined by one of the job evaluation methods and the
   a. skill-based pay plan.
   b. market-based wages.
   c. target wages or salary rates for the jobs in each pay grade.
   d. current average pay rates for your grades.

10. When employees are paid for acquiring new competencies and skill levels they achieve rather than based on the jobs they are assigned, the pay system is known as
    a. skill-based pay.
    b. broadbanding.
    c. wage reductions.
    d. pay grades.

11. The trend in compensation which involves collapsing salary grades and ranges into just a few wide levels or "bands," each of which contains a salary range of jobs and salary levels is referred to as
    a. skill-based pay.
    b. broadbanding.
    c. wage reductions.
    d. pay grades.

11. Company cars, yachts, and executive dining rooms are all examples of which type of executive compensation?
    a. short-term incentives
    b. benefits
    c. perquisites
    d. long-term incentives

13. Which of the following is the approach typically followed for evaluating professional jobs?
    a. point method
    b. factor comparison
    c. market-pricing
    d. ranking

14. The main issue in understanding comparable worth is
    a. how to pay employees in different jobs.
    b. should women who are performing jobs equal to men's or just comparable to men's be paid the same as men.
    c. should employees in different departments doing the same job be paid comparably.
    d. should all employees within the company be paid wages that are comparable.

15. Salary compression means that
    a. longer-term employees' salaries are lower than those for workers entering the firm today.
    b. longer-term employees' salaries are higher than those for workers entering the firm today.
    c. there is little difference between the salaries of employees in a pay grade.
    d. there is a lot of difference between the salaries of employees in a pay grade.

Essays

1. What is the Fair Labor Standards Act and what are its major provisions?

2. Briefly discuss the steps involved in establishing pay rates.

3. Compare and contrast the point method of job evaluation with the job classification method.

4. Describe two current trends in compensation, indicating advantages and disadvantages of each.

5. What are the major issues that must be addressed relative to top executive pay?

ANSWER KEY

Match Terms with Definitions

1. g   (p. 394)
2. a   (p. 394)
3. c   (p. 395)
4. h   (p. 395)
5. d   (p. 395)
6. f   (p. 398)
7. i   (p. 401)
8. b   (p. 402)
9. e   (p. 404)
10. j (p. 405)

True/False

1. F   (p. 394)
2. F   (p. 396)
3. T   (p. 396)
4. F   (p. 398-401)
5. F   (p. 403-405)
6. T   (p. 406)
7. T   (p. 406)
8. F   (p. 409-411)
9. T   (p. 417)
10. F (p. 417-418)
11. F (p. 419)
12. T (p. 421)

Multiple Choice

1. a   (p. 395)
2. b   (p. 395)
3. d   (p. 396)
4. c   (p. 401-402)
5. b   (p. 402)
6. d   (p. 402)
7. a   (p. 404)
8. c   (p. 406)
9. d   (p. 407)
10. a (p. 409)
11. b (p. 411)
12. c (p. 418)
13. c (p. 419)
14. b (p. 419)
15. a (p. 421)

Essay

1. Pages 395
2. Pages 398-409
3. Pages 404-405
4. Pages 409-413
5. Pages 417-419

CHAPTER 12

PAY-FOR-PERFORMANCE AND FINANCIAL INCENTIVES

CHAPTER DESCRIPTION

This chapter describes the various types of incentive plans used by organizations including short-term and long-term incentives. Guidelines are provided for how to implement incentive plans and suggestions as to why incentive plans don't work are provided.

CHAPTER OBJECTIVES

1. Discuss how to use piecework, standard hour, and team or group incentive plans.
2. Discuss how to use short-term and long-term incentives for managers and executives.
3. List the pros and cons of salary plans and commission plans for salespeople.
4. Explain how an incentive plan might backfire and how to avoid such a problem.

CHAPTER STUDY OUTLINE

I. Money and Motivation: Background
   A. Performance and pay
      1. Emphasis on shareholder-value
      2. Relationship between strategy and incentives
   B. Types of incentive plans
      1. Individual incentive programs
         a. Income over and above base salary
         b. Spot bonuses
      2. Group incentive programs
      3. Profit-sharing plans
      4. Variable pay

II. Incentives for Operations Employees
   A. Piecework plans
      1. Straight piecework plans
      2. Guaranteed piecework plans
      3. Advantages
         a. Simple to calculate and easily understood
         b. Appear equitable in principle
         c. Incentive value can be powerful because rewards directly tied to performance
      4. Disadvantages
         a. Unsavory reputation among some employees
         b. In workers' minds production standards become tied inseparably to amount of money earned
   B. Standard hour plan
   C. Team or group variable pay incentive plans
      1. Set work standards for each member of group
      2. Set production standard based on final ouput of group as a whole
      3. Choose measurable definition of group performance or productivity group can control
      4. Tie team performance to company's strategic goals
      5. Advantages
         a. Rewarding employees as a group encourages sense of cooperation
         b. Facilitate on-the-job training

  6. Disadvantage
    a. Each worker's rewards no longer based solely on his or her own efforts
    b. Free riders can be a problem

III. Incentives for Managers and Executives
 A. Short term incentives: The annual bonus
  1. Must decide how much to pay out (fund size)
   a. Nondeductible formula
   b. Deductible formula
  2. Deciding individual awards
   a. Split-award method
   b. Multiplier method
 B. Long-term incentives: Capital accumulation programs
  1. Stock option
  2. Other plans
   a. Stock appreciation rights
   b. Performance achievement plan
   c. Restricted stock plans
   d. Phantom stock plans
  3. Performance plans
  4. Long-term incentives: Cash vs. stock options
  5. Long-term incentives for overseas executives
  6. Relationship of strategy to executive compensation
   a. Define strategic context for executive compensation program
   b. Shape each component of package and group into balanced whole
   c. Create stock option plan to give package special character to meet unique needs of executives and company
   d. Check plan for compliance
   e. Install review and evaluation process

IV. Incentives for Salespeople
 A. Salary plan
  1. Advantages
   a. Salespeople know income in advance
   b. Employer has fixed, predictable sales force expenses
   c. Makes it simpler to switch territories or quotas or reassign salespeople
   d. Can lead to high degree of loyalty among sales staff
  2. Disadvantage – salary plans don't depend on results
 B. Commission plan
  1. Advantages
   a. Salespeople have greatest possible incentive
   b. Tendency to attract high-performing salespeople who see that effort will lead to rewards
   c. Sales costs proportional to sales
   d. Easy to understand and compute
  2. Disadvantages
   a. Focus is on making sale and on high-volume items
   b. Cultivating dedicated customers and working to push hard-to-sell items may be neglected
   c. Wide variances may occur in income of salespeople leading to feeling of inequity
   d. Salespeople encouraged to neglect nonselling duties like servicing small accounts
   e. Pay often excessive in boom times and low in recessions
 C. Combination plan

V. Incentives for Other Professionals and Employees
   A. Merit pay as an incentive
      1. Lump-sum merit payments
      2. Lump-sum merit pay based on both individual and organizational performance
   B. Incentives for professional employees

VI. Organizationwide Incentive Plans
   A. Profit-sharing plans
      1. Cash plans
      2. Deferred profit-sharing plans
   B. Employee stock ownership plan (ESOP)
   C. Scanlon plan
      1. Philosophy of cooperation
      2. Identity
      3. Competence
      4. Involvement system
      5. Sharing of benefits formula
      6. Conditions for success
         a. Relatively small number of participants
         b. Stable product lines and costs
         c. Good supervision and healthy labor relations essential
         d. Strong commitment to plan on part of both workers and management

   D. Gainsharing plans
      1. Implementation steps
         a. Establish general plan objectives
         b. Define specific performance measures
         c. Formulate funding formula
         d. Determine method for dividing and distributing employees' share of gains
         e. Make size of payment meaningful to get participants' attention and motivate their behavior
         f. Choose form of payment
         g. Decide how frequently bonuses are to be paid
         h. Develop support or involvement system
      2. Success factors
   E. At-risk variable pay plans

VII. Developing More Effective Incentive Plans
   A. When to use incentives
   B. How to implement incentive plans
      1. Link incentive with strategy
      2. Ensure effort and rewards directly related
      3. Make plan understandable and easily calculable by employees
      4. Set effective standards
      5. Guarantee your standards
      6. Guarantee an hourly base rate
      7. Get support for the plan
      8. Have good measurement systems
      9. Emphasize long-term as well as short-term success
      10. Take corporate culture into consideration
   C. Why incentive plans don't work
      1. Performance pay can't replace good management
      2. You get what you pay for

3. "Pay is not a motivator"
   4. Rewards punish
   5. Rewards rupture relationships
   6. Rewards can unduly restrict performance
   7. Rewards may undermine responsiveness
   8. Rewards undermine intrinsic motivation
   9. People work for more than money
D. Commitment and incentives
E. Incentive plans in practice

CHAPTER STUDY QUIZZES

Match Terms with Definitions

a. piecework
b. stock appreciation rights
c. standard hour plan
d. commission plan
e. profit sharing
f. deductible formula
g. variable pay
h. stock option
i. gainsharing plan
j. merit pay

_____ 1. Any plan that ties pay to productivity or to some other measure of the firm's profitability.

_____ 2. When earnings are tied directly to what the worker produces.

_____ 3. When the worker is rewarded by a percent premium that equals the percent by which his or her performance exceeds the standard.

_____ 4. When the short-term incentive fund begins to accumulate only after the firm has met a specified level of earnings.

_____ 5. The right to purchase a specific number of shares of company stock at a specific price during a period of time.

_____ 6. When the recipient can exercise the option (by buying the stock) or take any appreciation in the stock price in cash, stock, or some combination of these.

_____ 7. Pay for salespeople that is in direct proportion to their sales.

_____ 8. Any increase awarded to an employee based on his or her individual performance.

_____ 9. Plan in which all or most employees receive a share of the company's annual profits.

_____ 10. Incentive plan that engages many or all employees in a common effort to achieve a company's productivity objectives with any resulting incremental cost-savings gains shared among employees and company.

True/False

1. T F Merit pay is the oldest incentive plan and is still the most commonly used.

2. T F One advantage of the piecework plan is that the incentive value can be powerful because rewards are tied directly to performance.

3. T F Annual bonuses are designed to motivate the long-term performance of managers and executives.

4. T F In determining the amount of annual bonuses, typically a target bonus is set for each eligible position and adjustments are then made for greater or less than targeted performance.

5. T F Capital accumulation programs are usually available for all employees.

6. T F The strong emphasis in the past few years on corporate competitiveness and shareholder value creation as a performance indicator of corporate success has made more shareholders interested in emphasizing executive stock options over cash incentives.

7. T F Nonqualified stock options are options to purchase stock at a stated price, usually the fair market value at the time of the grant.

8. T F Restricted stock plans require that the executive pays the fair market value of the stock at the time it is sold.

9. T F The most prevalent approach for compensating salespeople is a combination of salary and commissions.

10. T F One problem with merit pay plans is their dependence on the validity of the performance appraisal system.

11. T F Employee stock ownership plans do not allow corporations to receive a tax deduction equal to the fair market value of the shares transferred to the trustee.

12. T F Scanlon plans are based on a philosophy of cooperation between managers and workers.

Multiple Choice

1. Bonuses generally awarded to individual employees for accomplishments that are not readily measured by a standard are referred to as
   a. spot bonuses.
   b. variable pay.
   c. lump-sum pay.
   d. merit pay.

2. The type of incentive plan in which earnings are tied directly to what the worker produces is known as
   a. piecework plan.
   b. guaranteed piecework. plan.
   c. skill-based pay.
   d. standard hour plan.

3. The type of incentive plan in which the worker is rewarded by a percent premium that equals the percent by which his or her performance exceeds the standard is known as the
   a. piecework plan.
   b. guaranteed piecework plan.
   c. skill-based plan.
   d. standard hour plan.

4. A major disadvantage of group incentive plans is that
   a. they aren't given frequently enough.
   b. employees don't understand how they are derived.
   c. each worker's rewards are no longer based solely on his or her own efforts.
   d. they provide no motivation for employees.

5. Team incentive plans are designed to reinforce which of the following behaviors?
   a. individual contributions to projects
   b. group planning and problem solving
   c. bickering among group members over who has "tight" production standards
   d. skill acquisition

6. When an organization uses a deductible formula to decide the total amount of bonus money that will be available, the organization is making which assumption?
   a. a straight percentage is used to create the short-term incentive fund
   b. a percentage plus approach is used to create the short-term incentive fund
   c. accumulation begins only after the firm has met a specified level of earnings
   d. accumulation begins at the start of each year

7. Individual annual bonuses are usually determined on the basis of
   a. setting a target bonus for each eligible position and making adjustments for greater or less than targeted performance.
   b. profit sharing percentages for all employees.
   c. setting a target bonus for each eligible employee and awarding that bonus amount, regardless of performance.
   d. gainsharing outcomes for the division in which the employee works.

8. _____ programs are usually reserved for senior general and functional area executives.
   a. Gainsharing.
   b. Profit sharing.
   c. Annual bonuses.
   d. Capital accumulation programs.

9. Which of the following trends has occurred relative to awarding stock options to employees?
   a. increasingly these options are limited to chief executive officers
   b. increasingly stock options are not just reserved for management personnel
   c. increasingly these options are not being offered to employees
   d. increasingly stock options are being phased out

10. The biggest advantage for awarding lump-sum merit raises rather than percentage increases to base wages is that
    a. the lump-sum merit raises are cumulative and, therefore, permanently impact base wages.
    b. the lump-sum merit raises are not cumulative and, therefore, significantly slow the rise in payroll expenses.
    c. lump-sum merit raises require less planning than percentage increases.
    d. lump-sum merit raises better reflect organizational profit-sharing.

11. In which type of profit-sharing plan do employees receive a percentage of profits distributed at regular intervals?
    a. Lincoln Incentive system
    b. deferred profit-sharing plan
    c. cash plan
    d. gainsharing

12. What does research suggest about employee stock ownership plans (ESOPs)?
    a. ESOPs encourage employees to develop a sense of ownership in and commitment to the firm
    b. ESOPs do not really encourage employees to develop a sense of ownership in and commitment to the firm
    c. ESOPs encourage employees to work harder only if they know they will get additional stock options
    d. ESOPs were effective only in the 1980s

13. The basic features of the Scanlon plan are
    a. employee ownership, competition, involvement
    b. philosophy of involvement and identity, sharing of benefits formula
    c. identity, involvement system, sharing of benefits formula
    d. philosophy of cooperation, identity, competence, involvement system, sharing of benefits formula

14. The basic difference among the various types of gainsharing plans is
    a. which employees are involved.
    b. the formula used to determine employee bonuses.
    c. who administers the plan.
    d. how long an employee has to work for a company to participate in the plan.

15. Incentive plans should be used when all but which of the following conditions exists?
    a. There is a clear relationship between employee effort and quantity or quality of output.
    b. When delays in the work are frequent and beyond employees' control.
    c. The job is standardized, the work flow is regular, and delays are few or consistent.
    d. Quality is less important than quantity, or, if quality is important, it too is easily measured and controlled.

Essays

1. What are some of the issues to consider when deciding on individual short-term incentives to pay to employees?

2. Describe the various types of capital accumulation programs available for executives.

3. What are the advantages and disadvantages to sales personnel of commission pay plans?

4. Briefly discuss the differences between profit sharing and gainsharing plans.

5. Why do incentive plans often not work?

ANSWER KEY

Match Terms with Definitions

1. g   (p. 438)
2. a   (p. 439)
3. c   (p. 440)
4. f   (p. 442)
5. h   (p. 443)

6. b   (p. 445)
7. d   (p. 448)
8. j   (p. 450)
9. e   (p. 452)
10. i (p. 456)

True/False

1. F (p. 439)	5. F (p. 443)	9. T (p. 447)
2. T (p. 439)	6. T (p. 443-444)	10. T (p. 451)
3. F (p. 441)	7. T (p. 444)	11. F (p. 453)
4. T (p. 442)	8. F (p. 445)	12. T (p. 455)

Multiple Choice

1. a (p. 438)	6. c (p. 442)	11. c (p. 453)
2. a (p. 439)	7. a (p. 442)	12. a (p. 454)
3. d (p. 440)	8. d (p. 443)	13. d (p. 455)
4. c (p. 440-441)	9. b (p. 444)	14. b (p. 457)
5. b (p. 441)	10. b (p. 451)	15. b (p. 458)

Essay

1. Page 442
2. Pages 443-445
3. Pages 448-449
4. Pages 452-457
5. Pages 459-461

CHAPTER 13

BENEFITS AND SERVICES

CHAPTER DESCRIPTION

This chapter describes the various types of benefits provided by employers--both mandatory and optional--and provides recommendations for reducing the costs of benefits to the employer.

CHAPTER OBJECTIVES

1. Describe each of the basic benefits most employers might be expected to offer.
2. Explain how to reduce an employer's unemployment insurance bill.
3. Explain why the cost of insurance benefits is increasing and identify what employers can do to reduce these costs.
4. Discuss how to set up a flexible benefits program.

CHAPTER STUDY OUTLINE

I. The Benefits Picture Today

II. Pay for Time Not Worked (Supplemental Pay Benefits)
   A. Unemployment insurance
      1. Provide for weekly benefits if person unable to work through some fault other than his or her own
      2. Benefits derive from unemployment tax on employers
      3. States each have their own unemployment laws
   B. Vacations and holidays
      1. Number of paid days varies from employer to employer
      2. Employers have to decide what wages employees receive while on paid vacation and if employees will get paid for accrued vacation time when leave company
      3. Also have to decide who will get holiday pay
   C. Sick leave
      1. Provides pay to employee out of work because of illness
      2. Some employers buy back unused sick leave to reduce abuse of sick leave
      3. Leave bank or paid time off (PTO) are other options
      4. Family and Medical Leave Act of 1993 (FMLA)
         a. Private employers of 50 or more employees must provide leave to eligible employees
         b. Employers may require employees to take any unused paid sick leave or annual leave as part of 12-week leave provided in law
         c. Employees taking leave entitled to receive health benefits while on unpaid leave
         d. Employers must guarantee employees' rights to return to previous or equivalent jobs
   D. Severance pay
   E. Supplemental unemployment benefits
      1. Paid by company
      2. Provide benefits above state employment compensation due to layoffs, reduced workweeks, and relocations
      3. Prevalent in collective bargaining agreements

III. Insurance Benefits
   A. Worker's compensation laws
      1. Aimed at providing prompt income and medical benefits to work-related accident victims or their

97

         dependents, regardless of fault
    2. Can be monetary or medical
    3. Usually handled by state administrative commissions
    4. Controlling worker's compensation costs
        a. Screen out accident-prone workers
        b. Reduce accidents and health problems that trigger these claims
        c. Institute rehabilitation programs for injured employees
        d. Use case management (treatment of injured workers on case-by-case basis by assigned medically trained manager such as registered nurse)
 B. Life insurance
 C. Hospitalization, medical, and disability insurance
    1. Aimed at providing protection against hospitalization costs and loss of income arising from accidents or illness occurring from off-the-job causes
    2. May include dental, vision, and accidental death and dismemberment coverage
    3. Health maintenance organizations (HMOs)
        a. Require that employees use HMO health care providers
        b. Receive fixed annual fee per employee from employer, regardless of whether or not service actually provided
    4. Preferred provider organizations (PPOs)
        a. Employees can choose health care providers from list
        b. Participating providers provide price discounts and submit to certain utilization controls
    5. Reducing health benefit costs
        a. Move away from 100 percent medical cost payments
        b. Increase annual deductibles
        c. Limit annual out-of-pocket medical expenses an employee pays
        d. Require medical contributions from employees
        e. Use gatekeepers
        f. Focus on health promotion and preventive health care
        g. Form health care coalitions
    6. AIDS
    7. Mental health benefits
    8. The Pregnancy Discrimination Act (PDA)
    9. COBRA requirements
    10. Long-term care

IV. Retirement Benefits
 A. Social security
 B. Pension plans
    1. Defined benefit pension plan uses formula for determining retirement benefits so that actual benefits are defined ahead of time
    2. Defined contribution plan specified what contribution the employer will make to a retirement or savings fund set up for employee
        a. Savings and thrift plans [e.g., 401(k)] require employees to contribute portion of their earnings which is matched in whole or part by employer
        b. Deferred profit-sharing plans involve employers contributing portion of profits to pension fund regardless of employee contributions
        c. Employee stock ownership plans are qualified, tax-deductible stock bonus plans in which employers contribute stock to a trust for eventual use by employees
    3. Policy issues
        a. Membership requirements
        b. Benefit formula
        c. Plan-funding
        d. Vesting

  4. Portability
 C. Pensions and the law
  1. Employee Retirement Income Security Act (ERISA)
  2. Pension Benefit Guarantee Corporation (PBGC)
 D. Benefits trends: Golden offerings in form of early retirement windows

V. Employee Services Benefits
 A. Personal services benefits
  1. Credit unions
  2. Counseling services
  3. Employee Assistance Programs (EAPS)
  4. Other personal services
   a. Lakefront vacations
   b. Weight loss programs
   c. Cultural subsidy
   d. Lunch-and-learn program
 B. Job-related services benefits
  1. Subsidized child care
  2. Elder care
  3. Subsidized employee transportation\
  4. Food services
  5. Educational subsidies
  6. Family friendly benefits
  7. Rationale for offering based on research
   a. Strong and negative relationship between job satisfaction and various work-family conflict measures
   b. Strong negative correlation between work-family conflict and measures of "life satisfaction"
   c. Managers need to recognize importance of family-friendly benefits
 C. Executive perquisites

VI. Flexible Benefits Programs
 A. Employee preferences for various benefits
  1. Influenced by marital status, age, and gender
  2. Employees do prefer flexibility in benefits
 B. Cafeteria approach
  1. Give employees benefits fund budget and lets them choose how to spend that within guidelines
  2. Advantage is flexibility
  3. Disadvantage is substantial clerical and administrative costs

CHAPTER STUDY QUIZZES

Match Terms with Definitions

a. unemployment insurance
b. vesting
c. health maintenance organization
d. severance pay
e. defined benefit pension plan

f. sick leave
g. worker's compensation
h. preferred provider organization
i. social security
j. defined contribution benefit plan

_____ 1. Provides weekly benefits if a person is unable to work through some fault other than his or her own

_____ 2. Provides pay to an employee when he or she is out of work because of illness.

_____ 3. Provides a one-time payment made when terminating an employee.

_____ 4. Provides sure, prompt income and medical benefits to work-related accident victims or their dependents, regardless of fault.

_____ 5. Medical organization consisting of several specialists operating out of a community-based health care center, providing round-the-clock medical services at a specific site to employees who pay a nominal fee.

_____ 6. Groups of health care providers that contract with employers, insurance companies, or third-party payers to provide medical care services at a reduced fee.

_____ 7. Provides retirement income, survivor's benefits, death benefits, and disability payments.

_____ 8. Uses a formula to determine retirement benefits so that actual benefits to be received are defined ahead of time.

_____ 9. Specifies what contribution the employer will make to a retirement or savings fund set up for the employee.

_____ 10. Process designed to ensure that the employee will get monies set aside by the employer for the employee's retirement.

True/False

1. T F An employer's unemployment tax rate reflects its rate of personnel terminations.

2. T F The Family and Medical Leave Act of 1993 (FMLA) applies only to females.

3. T F Supplemental unemployment benefits are designed to offset economic loss due to layoffs, reduced workweeks, and relocations.

4. T F Worker's compensation is usually handled by federal government administrative commissions.

5. T F Worker's compensation costs can be reduced by assigning a professional the task of coordinating and overseeing the worker's rehabilitation and gradual reassimilation into the firm's workforce.

6. T F Most private employers are not required to make continued health benefits available to terminated or retired employees.

7. T F In deferred profit-sharing plans, employers typically contribute a portion of their profits to the pension fund, regardless of the level of employee contribution.

8. T F The purpose of the Pension Guarantee Corporation is to ensure that pensions meet vesting obligations and to insure pensions should a plan terminate without sufficient funds to meet its vested obligations.

9. T F Age discrimination is not a concern when establishing early retirement programs.

10. T F Employee assistance programs are formal programs designed to provide employees with counseling and/or treatment for problems such as alcoholism, gambling, or stress.

11. T F   Subsidized daycare centers have been found to be associated with increased ability to attract employees, lower absenteeism, improve morale, and lower turnover.

12. T F   Under flexible benefits plans employers give each employee a benefits fund budget and let the person spend that on whichever benefits he or she prefers with no constraints.

Multiple Choice

1. Unemployment insurance benefits are designed for which group of employees?
   a. all dismissed employees
   b. only employees terminated through no fault of their own
   c. only employees whose behavior causes them to be terminated
   d. only employees who have been laid off from their jobs

2. One way to cut unemployment insurance costs is to
   a. save money by not having exit interviews.
   b. let managers and supervisors make decisions however they want to about employee terminations since they know employee performance best.
   c. verify unemployment claims.
   d. trust that the audit statement is correct.

3. All but which of the following are ways employers have tried to reduce the problem of employees abusing sick leave?
   a. buying back unused sick leave at the end of the year
   b. holding monthly lotteries of cash prizes for employees with perfect monthly attendance
   c. investigating all absences
   d. doing away with sick leave

4. The Family and Medical Leave Act provides up to 12 weeks of unpaid leave for eligible employees under which circumstance?
   a. employee's own serious illness
   b. birth or adoption of a child
   c. care of seriously ill child, spouse, or parent
   d. all of the above

5. Under worker's compensation, an employee must prove that the injury
   a. arose while the employee was on the job.
   b. arose while the employee was on the job and it was not the employee's fault.
   c. did not occur out of employee negligence.
   d. occurred while the employee was following all safety guidelines.

6. Accidental death and dismemberment insurance coverage provides
   a. a percentage of the policy value to eligible employees.
   b. only a life insurance benefit to eligible employees.
   c. a fixed lump-sum benefit in addition to life insurance benefits when death is accidental.
   d. a fixed lump-sum benefit only.

7. Unlike health maintenance organizations, preferred provider organizations
   a. require that employees live in HMO-designated service areas.
   b. require no copayment.
   c. let employees select providers (such as participating doctors).
   d. cover doctor and hospital bills if approved.

8. The Pregnancy Discrimination Act requires that employers treat women affected by pregnancy, childbirth, or related medical conditions
    a. the same as any employee not able to work, with respect to benefits, including sick leave and disability benefits, and health and medical insurance.
    b. the same as any employee not able to work only with respect to sick leave.
    c. on a case by case basis in terms of benefits.
    d. the same as any other terminated employee..

9. Social security benefits include
    a. retirement income and survivor's or death benefits.
    b. retirement income.
    c. retirement income and disability payments.
    d. retirement income, survivor's or death benefits, and disability payments.

10. What is the major advantage of a 401(k) plan?
    a. Allows a pretax reduction in salary, so the employee isn't taxed on those set-aside dollars until after he or she retires or removes the money from the pension fund
    b. It is easier to administer than other pension plans
    c. Only executives are allowed to participate in the plan, thus, reducing costs to the employer
    d. It is an after tax plan so the employee won't have to worry about paying taxes when he or she retires

11. Pension funds that are _____ allow the employee to take their retirement income when they leave the company and roll it over into a new employer's savings plan or IRA.
    a. vested
    b. funded
    c. deferred
    c. portable

12. One problem that gets employers in trouble when they offer early retirement windows is whether or not the program is truly
    a. available.
    b. funded.
    c. voluntary.
    d. enforceable.

13. To ensure the success of an employee assistance program, employers should do all but which of the following?
    a. specify goals and philosophy
    b. be aware of legal issues
    c. ensure professional staffing
    d. share information with managers

14. A main problem with implementing family-friendly benefits seems to be employees' reluctance to use them because
    a. most employees don't need them.
    b. they think managers will frown upon those who use the programs.
    c. of the concern over how coworkers will perceive them if they use the benefits.
    d. they aren't advertised well.

15. The main advantage of a flexible benefits program is that it allows
    a. employees to develop individualized benefits packages for themselves by choosing the benefit options they prefer.
    b. the company to save money by not giving employees benefits that they don't need or want.
    c. employees to buy benefits from each other.
    d. the company to monitor just what benefits employees have.

Essays

1. Discuss how employers can cut unemployment insurance costs.

2. How can an employer reduce health benefit costs?

3. Discuss the policy issues employers must address relative to pension plans.

4. Describe three types of personal services benefits offered by employers.

5. What are the advantages and disadvantages of flexible benefits programs?

ANSWER KEY

Match Terms with Definitions

1. a   (p. 475)
2. f   (p. 479)
3. d   (p. 481)
4. g   (p. 481)
5. c   (p. 483)
6. h   (p. 486)
7. i   (p. 486)
8. e   (p. 489)
9. j   (p. 489)
10. b (p. 490)

True/False

1. T (p. 475)
2. F (p. 479)
3. T (p. 481-482)
4. F (p. 483)
5. T (p. 484)
6. F (p. 488)
7. T (p. 490)
8. T (p. 491)
9. F (p. 492)
10. T (p. 493)
11. T (p. 495)
12. F (p. 499)

Multiple Choice

1. b (p. 475)
2. c (p. 477-478)
3. d (p. 479)
4. d (p. 479)
5. a (p. 483)
6. c (p. 485)
7. c (p. 486)
8. a (p. 488)
9. d (p. 489)
10. a (p. 490)
11. d (p. 491)
12. c (p. 492-493)
13. d (p. 494)
14. b (p. 497)
15. a (p. 498)

Essay

1. Pages 477-478
2. Pages 486-487
3. Pages 490-491
4. Pages 493-494
5. Pages 499-500

CHAPTER 14

LABOR RELATIONS AND COLLECTIVE BARGAINING

CHAPTER DESCRIPTION

This chapter discusses the history of the labor movement and why workers unionize, the laws that affect the unionization process, how union drives and elections take place, and what companies should do in managing in a union environment.

CHAPTER OBJECTIVES

1. Describe the history of the labor movement and why workers unionize.
2. Discuss in detail the nature of the major federal labor relations laws.
3. Describe the process of a union drive and election.
4. Explain how to avoid losing a unionization election.
5. Describe the nature of the collective bargaining process.
6. List important do's and don'ts for handling grievances.

CHAPTER STUDY OUTLINE

I. Introduction: The Labor Movement
   A. A brief history of the American union movement
      1. Skilled craftsmen organized themselves into trade unions as early as 1790
      2. Membership grew until major depression around 1837
      3. Membership increased during industrial revolution
      4. Knights of Labor formed by group of tailors in 1869 and dissolved in 1893
      5. American Federation of Labor (AFL) formed in 1886 by Samuel Gompers
      6. Membership in AFL exceeded 5.5 million after World War I
      7. 1920s period of stagnation for U. S. union movement
      8. Membership increased again in mid-1930s
      9. Organized labor's share of workforce in U. S. today is about 14.1 percent and dropping
   B. Why do workers organize?
      1. Basic bread-and-butter issues
      2. Dissatisfaction with issues such as job security and wages most strongly correlated with vote for union
      3. Belief that only through unionization can workers get their fair share of the pie and protect themselves from whims of management
   C. What do unions want?
      1. Union security
         a. Closed shop – company can hire only union members
         b. Union shop – company can hire nonunion people but they must join union after a prescribed period of time and pay dues
         c. Agency shop – nonunion employees must pay union dues
         d. Open shop – up to workers whether or not to join union
         e. Maintenance of membership arrangement – no required union membership but union members employed by firm have to maintain union membership for contract period
      2. Improved wages, hours, and benefits for members
   D. The AFL-CIO
      1. What it is
         a. American Federation of Labor and Congress of Industrial Organizations
         b. Voluntary federation of about 100 national and international labor unions in the U. S.

2. Structure of AFL-CIO
   a. Local union
   b. National union
   c. National federation

II. Unions and the Law
   A. Background
      1. No special labor laws until about 1930
      2. Labor law has since gone through three clear changes
   B. Period of strong encouragement: The Norris-LaGuardia Act (1932) and the National Labor Relations or Wagner Act (1935)
      1. Norris-LaGuardia Act
         a. Guaranteed to each employee right to bargain collectively "free from interference, restraint, or coercion"
         b. Declared yellow dog contracts unenforceable
         c. Limited courts' abilities to issue injunctions for activities such as peaceful picketing and payment of strike benefits
      2. National Labor Relations (or Wagner) Act of 1935
         a. Banned certain unfair labor practices
         b. Provided secret-ballot elections and majority rule for determining whether a firm's employees were to unionize
         c. Created National Labor Relations Board (NLRB) for enforcing above two provisions
      3. Unfair employer labor practices per Wagner Act
         a. Unfair for employers to "interfere with, restrain, or coerce employees" in exercising legally sanctioned right to organize
         b. Unfair practice for company representatives to dominate or interfere with either formation or administration of labor unions
         c. Companies prohibited from discriminating against employees for legal union activities
         d. Employers forbidden to discharge or discriminate against employees because they file unfair practice charges against the company
         e. Unfair labor practice for employers to refuse to bargain collectively with employees' duly chosen representatives
      4. From 1935 to 1947 union membership increased quickly
   C. Period of modified encouragement coupled with regulation: The Taft-Hartley Act (1947)
      1. Limited unions
         a. Prohibited unfair union labor practices
         b. Enumerated rights of employees as union members
         c. Enumerated rights of employers
         d. Allowed president of U. S. to temporarily bar national emergency strikes
      2. Unfair labor practices
         a. Unions banned from restraining or coercing employees from exercising their guaranteed bargaining rights
         b. Unfair labor practice for unions to cause employers to discriminate in any way against employee to discourage or encourage union membership
         c. Unfair for unions to refuse to bargain in good faith with employer about wages, hours, and other employment conditions
         d. Unfair for unions to engage in featherbedding (requiring employer to pay employee for services not performed)
      3. Rights of employees
      4. Rights of employers
      5. National emergency strike
   D. Period of detailed regulation of internal union affairs: The Landrum-Griffin Act (1959)
      1. Contains a bill of rights for union members
      2. Laid out rules regarding union elections

3. Expanded list of unlawful employer actions

E. Labor law today
1. *Jean Country* case
2. *TWA v. Independent Federation of Flight Attendants*

III. The Union Drive and Election
A. Steps in unionization process
1. Step 1. Initial contact
a. Labor relations consultants
b. Union salting
2. Step 2. Obtaining authorization cards
a. What management can do
b. What unions can do
3. Step 3. Hold a hearing
a. Consent election can be held immediately if employer does not contest union recognition
b. If employer contests, NLRB is contacted by union, which requests a hearing
(1) Does record indicate enough evidence to hold an election?
(2) RD must decide what will be bargaining unit
(3) Employer can challenge decision
c. If results of hearing are favorable for union, NLRB directs that election be held
4. Step 4. The campaign
5. Step 5. The election
B. How to lose an NLRB election
1. Reason 1. Asleep at the switch
2. Reason 2. Appointing a committee
3. Reason 3. Concentrating on money and benefits
4. Reason 4. Industry blind spots
5. Reason 5. Delegating too much to division or branches
C. The supervisor's role
D. Rules regarding literature and solicitation
E. Guidelines for employers wishing to stay union-free
1. Practice preventive employee relations
2. Recognize the importance of location
3. Seek early detection
4. Do not volunteer
5. Beware of the authorization cards
6. Present your case
7. Postpone the election
8. Pick your time carefully
9. Consider your options
F. Decertification elections: When employees want to oust their union

IV. The Collective Bargaining Process
A. What is collective bargaining?
B. What is good faith?
1. Good faith—cornerstone of effective labor management relations
2. When is bargaining not in good faith?
a. Surface bargaining
b. Inadequate concessions
c. Inadequate proposals and demands
d. Dilatory tactics
e. Imposing conditions
f. Making unilateral changes in conditions
g. Bypassing the representative
h. Committing unfair labor practices during negotiations

            i. Withholding information
            j. Ignoring bargaining items
    C. The negotiating team
    D. Bargaining items
        1. Voluntary bargaining items
        2. Illegal bargaining items
        3. Mandatory items
    E. Bargaining stages
        1. Hints on bargaining
        2. Trust-building behaviors
    F. Impasses, mediation, and strikes
        1. Impasse defined
        2. Third-party involvement
            a. Mediation
            b. Arbitration
        3. Strikes
            a. Economic strike
            b. Unfair labor practice strikes
            c. Wildcat strike
            d. Sympathy strike
        4. Preparing for the strike
        5. Other alternatives
            a. Boycott
            b. Inside games
            c. Lockout
    G. The contract agreement itself
    H. Changes to expect after being unionized

V. Contract Administration: Grievances
    A. The important role of contract administration
    B. What are the sources of grievance?
    C. The grievance procedure
    D. Guidelines for handling grievances
        1. Developing the proper environment
        2. Some guidelines: Do's and don'ts

VI. The Future of Unionism
    A. Unions fall on hard times
    B. What's next for unions?
    C. Unions and employee participation programs
    D. Are employee participation programs unfair labor practices?
        1. "Safe" participation programs
        2. Modern operating agreements

CHAPTER STUDY QUIZZES

Match Terms with Definitions

a. union shop
b. bargaining unit
c. arbitration
d. Taft-Hartley Act
e. open shop

f. Wagner Act
g. Landrum-Griffin Act
h. mediation
i. agency shop
j. lockout

_____ 1. The company can hire nonunion people but they must join the union after a prescribed period of time and pay dues.

_____ 2. Employees who do not belong to the union still must pay union dues on the assumption that the union's efforts benefit all workers.

_____ 3. It is up to the workers whether or not they join the union—those who do not, do not pay dues.

_____ 4. Act that identified unfair employer labor practices.

_____ 5. Act that enumerated several labor practices that unions were prohibited from engaging in.

_____ 6. Act that protected union members from possible wrongdoing on the part of their unions.

_____ 7. The group of employees that the union will be authorized to represent and bargain for collectively.

_____ 8. Using a neutral third party who tries to assist the principals in reaching agreement.

_____ 9. The most definitive type of third-party intervention where the third party has the power to determine and dictate the settlement terms.

_____ 10. A refusal by the employer to provide opportunities to work.

True/False

1. T F The urge to unionize often boils down to the belief that it is only through unity that the workers can get their fair share of the pie and also protect themselves from the arbitrary whims of management.

2. T F The AFL-CIO is made up of two layers: the local union and the national union.

3. T F The Norris-LaGuardia Act defined five unfair labor practices used by employers.

4. T F Union organizers can tell antiunion employees that they will lose their jobs if they don't join the union.

5. T F The president of the United States can intervene in national emergency strikes.

6. T F Thirty percent of the eligible employees in an appropriate bargaining unit must sign authorization cards before an election can be petitioned.

7. T F Most companies do not contest the union's right to represent their employees.

8. T F One sure way an employer can lose a union election is to delegate too much to divisions or branches.

9. T F Once a union has become certified through an election the union will always be part of that company.

10. T F Bargaining in good faith means that both parties communicate and negotiate, that proposals are matched with counterproposals, and that both parties make every reasonable effort to arrive at an agreement.

11. T F Voluntary bargaining items become part of negotiations only through the joint agreement of both management and the union.

12. T F A sympathy strike occurs when one union strikes in support of the strike of another union.

Multiple Choice

1. In this type of shop, the company can hire nonunion people but those individuals must join the union after a prescribed period of time and pay dues or they can be fired.
   a. closed shop
   b. union shop
   c. agency shop
   d. open shop

2. This Act banned certain unfair labor practices, provided for secret-ballot elections and majority rule for determining whether a firm's employees were to unionize, and created the National Labor Relations Board.
   a. Norris-LaGuardia Act
   b. Wagner Act
   c. Taft-Hartley Act
   d. Landrum-Griffin Act

3. This Act limited unions by prohibiting unfair union labor practices, enumerating the rights of employees as union members, enumerating the rights of employers, and allows the president of the United States to temporarily bar national emergency strikes.
   a. Norris-LaGuardia Act
   b. Wagner Act
   c. Taft-Hartley Act
   d. Landrum-Griffin Act

4. This Act was designed to protect union members from possible wrongdoing on the part of their unions and amended the National Labor Relations Act.
   a. Norris-LaGuardia Act
   b. Wagner Act
   c. Taft-Hartley Act
   d. Landrum-Griffin Act

5. The initiative for the first contact between the employees and the union may come from
   a. the employees.
   b. a union already representing other employees of the firm.
   c. a union representing workers elsewhere.
   d. all of the above.

6. The union organizing tactic by which workers who are in fact employed full-time by a union as undercover union organizers are hired by unwitting employers is known as
   a. union salting.
   b. boycotting.
   c. lockout.
   d. arbitration.

7. All but which of the following can occur once authorization cards have been collected?
   a. the employer can choose not to contest union recognition, no hearing is needed, and a "consent election" is held immediately
   b. the employer can choose not to contest the union's right to an election and/or the scope of the bargaining unit, and/or which employees are eligible, no hearing is needed, and the parties can stipulate an election
   c. the employer can contest the union's right and insist on a hearing to determine those issues
   d. the employer can contest the union's right and refuse a hearing

8. The supervisor's role in the unionization process is to
   a. actively prevent any unionization efforts.
   b. covertly prevent any unionization efforts.
   c. be knowledgeable about what they can and can't do to legally hamper organizing activities.
   d. be knowledgeable of the latest guerilla warfare tactics for preventing unionization.

9. One thing that employers can do to try to stay union free is to
   a. focus on tasks at hand and not worry about the possibility of unionization.
   b. let the union decide when to hold the election.
   c. practice preventive employee relations.
   d. locate operations in the northern states such as Michigan.

10. Wages, hours, rest periods, and layoffs fall under which category of bargaining items?
    a. mandatory
    b. permissible
    c. illegal
    d. voluntary

11. A/an _____ occurs when the parties are not able to move further toward settlement of a union contract.
    a. boycott
    b. lockout
    c. impasse
    d. shutdown

12. A strike that occurs during the term of a union contract is referred to as a/an
    a. economic strike.
    b. unfair labor practice strike.
    c. sympathy strike.
    d. wildcat strike..

13. A refusal by an employer to provide opportunities to work is known as a
    a. boycott.
    b. wildcat strike.
    c. economic strike.
    d. lockout.

14. The process by which various contract clauses gain meaning and the contract becomes a living document is the _____ procedure.
    a. arbitration
    b. grievance
    c. mediation
    d. impasse

15. One trend among unions is that they are
    a. seeking ownership and control of corporations.
    b. becoming less aggressive and less sophisticated in how they present themselves to the public.
    c. focusing only on blue-collar workers.
    d. totally supportive of employee participation programs.

Essays

1. Outline the history of the union movement in the U. S. and discuss its current status.

2. Discuss the major emphases of each piece of legislation that deals with union issues.

3. Describe the process that unions must go through to be recognized to represent employees.

4. What must management avoid if the company does not want to lose a NLRB election?

5. Discuss what it means to bargain in good faith.

ANSWER KEY

Match Terms with Definitions

1. a (p. 518)
2. i (p. 518)
3. e (p. 518)
4. f (p. 519)
5. d (p. 520)
6. g (p. 522)
7. b (p. 528)
8. h (p. 540)
9. c (p. 540)
10. j (p. 541)

True/False

1. T (p. 516)
2. F (p. 518)
3. F (p. 519)
4. F (p. 520)
5. T (p. 522)
6. T (p. 527)
7. F (p. 528-531)
8. T (p. 533)
9. F (p. 535-536)
10. T (p. 536-537)
11. T (p. 538)
12. T (p. 540)

Multiple Choice

1. b (p. 518)
2. b (p. 519)
3. c (p. 520)
4. d (p. 522)
5. d (p. 526)
6. a (p. 526-527)
7. d (p. 528)
8. c (p. 533)
9. c (p. 534)
10. a (p. 538)
11. c (p. 539)
12. d (p. 540)
13. d (p. 541)
14. b (p. 543-546)
15. a (p. 547)

Essay

1. Pages 515-516, 546-548
2. Pages 519-524
3. Pages 525-531
4. Pages 532-533
5. Pages 536-537

CHAPTER 15

EMPLOYEE SAFETY AND HEALTH

CHAPTER DESCRIPTION

This chapter describes the Occupational and Safety Act, employer responsibility for workplace safety, causes of accidents at work, and other major health problems that affect employees. Recommendations are provided for remedying these problems.

CHAPTER OBJECTIVES

1. Discuss OSHA and how it operates.
2. Describe the supervisor's role in safety.
3. Explain in detail three basic causes of accidents.
4. Explain in detail how to prevent accidents at work.
5. Discuss major health problems at work and how to remedy them.

CHAPTER STUDY OUTLINE

I. Why Employee Safety and Health Are Important
    A. Staggering number of work-related accidents
    B. Human suffering incurred by injured workers and their families
    C. Economic costs incurred by specific employers

II. Basic Facts About Occupational Safety Law
    A. Purpose of Occupational Safety and Health Act is to assure safe and healthful working conditions and to preserve human resources
    B. Administered by Occupational Safety and Health Administration (OSHA)
    C. OSHA standards
    D. OSHA recordkeeping procedures
    E. Inspections and citations
        1. Inspection priorities
            a. Imminent danger
            b. Catastrophes, fatalities, and accidents that have already occurred
            c. Valid employee complaints of alleged violations of standards
            d. Periodic special-emphasis inspections aimed at high-hazard industries, occupations, or substances
            e. Random inspections and reinspections
        2. Inspection itself
            a. Inspector arrives, explains visit, scope of inspection and standards that apply
            b. Authorized employee representative given opportunity to accompany inspector
            c. Inspector holds closing conference with employer's representative
        3. Citations and penalties
    F. Responsibilities and rights of employers and employees
        1. Dealing with employee resistance
        2. Reducing liability
    G. Changing nature of OSHA
        1. Changes in reporting requirements
        2. Reform bills
        3. More technologically advanced

III. The Supervisor's Role in Safety
    A. Top management commitment

  B. First-line supervisor

IV. What Causes Accidents?
  A. Unsafe conditions and other work-related accident-causing factors
    1. Unsafe conditions need to be eliminated or minimized
    2. Job itself
    3. Work schedule
    4. Psychological climate
  B. Personal characteristics that characterize "accident-prone" people and accidents
    1. Traits
    2. Vision
    3. Age
    4. Perceptual versus motor skills
    5. Vocational interests

V. How to Prevent Accidents
  A. Reducing unsafe conditions
  B. Reducing unsafe acts through selection and placement
    1. Identify human traits related to accidents on specific job in question
    2. ADA and safety
  C. Reducing unsafe acts through posters and other propaganda
  D. Reducing unsafe acts through training
  E. Reducing unsafe acts through incentive programs and positive reinforcement
    1. The new safety program
    2. Reinforcement and safety
  F. Reducing unsafe acts through top-management commitment
  G. Emphasize safety
  H. Establish a safety policy
  I. Set specific loss control goals
  J. Conduct safety and health inspections regularly
  K. Monitor work overload and stress
  L. Safety beyond the plant gate
  M. Controlling worker's compensation costs

VI. Employee Health: Problems and Remedies
  A. Alcoholism and substance abuse
    1. Traditional techniques used to deal with these problems
      a. Substance abuse testing
      b. In-house counseling
      c. Supervisory training/company policy
      d. Administering urine tests
      e. Conducting workplace inspections
      f. Using undercover agents
    2. Workplace substance abuse and the law
  B. The problems of job stress and burnout
    1. Environmental stressors
    2. Personal stressors
    3. Reducing job stress
      a. Develop awareness
      b. Adjust attitudes
      c. Take action
  C. Burnout
    1. Break your patterns
    2. Get away from it all periodically
    3. Reassess your goals in terms of your intrinsic worth
    4. Think about your work

D. Asbestos exposure at work
   E. Video display health problems and how to avoid them
   F. AIDS and the workplace
   G. Workplace smoking
      1. Nature of the problem
      2. What you can and cannot do
      3. Smoking policies
   H. Dealing with violence at work
      1. Nature of the problem
      2. Reducing incidents of workplace violence
         a. Heightened security measures
         b. Improved employee screening
         c. Workplace violence training
         d. Enhanced attention to retaining employees
      3. Dealing with angry employees
      4. Legal constraints on reducing workplace violence

CHAPTER STUDY QUIZZES

Match Terms with Definitions

a. penalty
b. Occupational Safety and Health Act
c. citations
d. unsafe conditions
e. burnout
f. OSHA
g. role overload
h. inspection
i. imminent danger
j. special-emphasis inspections

_____ 1. The Act passed by Congress in 1970 "to assure so far as possible every working man and woman in the nation safe and healthful working conditions and to preserve our human resources."

_____ 2. Office that administers the Occupational Safety and Health Act.

_____ 3. Process used by OSHA to determine if employers are in violation of safety standards.

_____ 4. Conditions in which it is likely that a danger exists that can immediately cause death or serious physical harm.

_____ 5. Inspections of catastrophes, fatalities, and accidents that have occurred.

_____ 6. Method used to inform employer and employees of the regulations and standards that have been violated and of the time limit set for rectifying the problem.

_____ 7. Fine imposed upon employers charged with OSHA violations.

_____ 8. One main cause of work-related accidents includes such factors as improperly guarded equipment, defective equipment, and improper ventilation.

_____ 9. The degree to which the employee's performance is seen as being affected by inadequate time, training, and resources.

_____ 10. The total depletion of physical and mental resources caused by excessive striving to reach an unrealistic work-related goal.

True/False

1. T F   The enforcement agency for the Occupational Safety and Health Act is the Office of Federal Contract Compliance Programs.
2. T F   All employers must maintain records of occupational injuries and illnesses.
3. T F   The top priority on OSHA's list of inspection priorities is catastrophes, fatalities, and accidents that have already occurred.
4. T F   An authorized employee representative is given an opportunity to accompany the OSHA officer during the inspection of the workplace.
5. T F   OSHA calculates penalties based on the seriousness of a particular violation without regard to the size of the business, the firm's compliance history, and the employer's good faith.
6. T F   Courts have typically not held employers liable for safety violations at the workplace if the violation occurred because the employee resisted following safety precautions and procedures.
7. T F   Work schedules and fatigue affect accident rates.
8. T F   Experts believe that individuals who are accident prone on one job may not be accident prone on another job.
9. T F   Because of the ADA, employers can no longer inquire about an applicant's worker's compensation history.
10. T F   Alcoholism can cause both the quality and quantity of work to decline although the alcoholic probably won't have a greater incidence of on-the-job accidents than other workers.
11. T F   Companies are required to monitor the air only when an employer expects the level of asbestos to have risen to the allowable limit.
12. T F   Homicide is the second leading cause of job-related deaths.

Multiple Choice

1. OSHA requires reporting of which of the following information?
    a. both occupational injuries and occupational illnesses
    b. only occupational injuries
    c. only occupational illnesses
    d. only occupational injuries that result in death or loss of body parts

2. OSHA conducts most of its workplace inspections as a result of
    a. learning through the media that an incident has occurred at a workplace.
    b. employee complaints.
    c. a regular list that is kept of past offenders.
    d. a random selection process.

3. Once the inspection has been completed, the inspector
    a. returns to his or her office and writes up a report to file.
    b. meets with all of the employees in the company affected by the reason for the inspection.
    c. sends a report only to the employee who complained.
    d. holds a closing conference with the employer's representative.

4. What are employers required by law to do when they receive a citation indicating a violation of OSHA standards?
    a. mail a copy of the citation to all employees
    b. publish the information from the citation in the employee newlsetter
    c. post the citation at or near the place where the violation occurred
    d. have the citation available if an employee wants to review it

5. The purpose of the two OSHA reform bills signed by President Clinton in 1998 was to help OSHA
    a. focus on achieving its aims through cooperation rather than through confrontation.
    b. have more leverage when employers were found to be noncompliant.
    c. obtain more employees so that more inspections can be conducted.
    d. have the resources to review all employers regularly.

6. Which of the following is not one of the three basic causes of accidents?
    a. unsafe conditions
    b. accident-prone personality
    c. unsafe acts
    d. chance occurrences

7. An example of an unsafe act in the workplace would be
    a. operating or working at unsafe speeds
    b. improperly guarded equipment
    c. hazardous procedures in, on, or around machines or equipment
    d. improper ventilation

8. Which of the following is not suggested as a selection technique aimed at reducing accident occurrence?
    a. measures of muscular coordination
    b. employee reliability tests
    c. emotional stability and personality tests
    d. using age as a selection criterion

9. The reason programs such as incentives increase workplace safety is that they focus on
    a. punishing unsafe behaviors.
    b. positive reinforcement.
    c. extinction of unsafe behaviors.
    d. negative reinforcement.

10. The best way to reduce worker's compensation costs is to
    a. begin to control these costs before the accident happens by taking preventive measures.
    b. not hire someone who has a record of worker's compensation claims.
    c. constantly remind employees of how much these costs are for the company.
    d. make workers pay for their own medical treatment.

11. The law which requires that employers with federal government contracts or grants eliminate alcohol and substance abuse on the job is the
    a. Americans with Disabilities Act.
    b. Occupational Safety and Health Act.
    c. Drug-Free Workplace Act.
    d. Civil Rights Act of 1991.

12. What are the two main causes of job stress?
    a. environmental factors such as work schedules
    b. incompetent managers and difficult tasks
    c. personal factors such as personality type
    d. both a and c

13. Common complaints among video display operators include all but which of the following?
    a. eye problems like burning, itching and tearing
    b. carpal tunnel syndrome
    c. eyestrain
    d. eye soreness

14. Which of the following can you legally do with regards to denying a job to a smoker?
    a. You can deny the applicant the job as long as the denial is not a surrogate for some other kind of discrimination.
    b. You cannot legally deny a job to a smoker.
    c. You can require the person to quit smoking as a condition of employment.
    d. You can require a physical exam of his/her propensity for lung cancer.

15. If an employer wants to reduce violence in the workplace, which of the following actions can it take?
    a. improved employee screening
    b. workplace violence training
    c. heightened security measures
    d. all of the above

Essays

1. Discuss the purpose of the Occupational Safety and Health Act.

2. Describe OSHA's inspection priorities and why it is necessary for OSHA to prioritize inspections.

3. What are the three basic causes of accidents and what can employers do to reduce the likelihood of occurrence?

3. How can employers address the issue of alcoholism and substance abuse in the workplace?

5. Describe three other types of workplace health issues an employer should be aware of and what can be done to address those issues.

ANSWER KEY

Match Terms with Definitions

1. b (p. 561)
2. f (p. 561)
3. h (p. 562-563)
4. i (p. 562)
5. j (p. 562)
6. c (p. 565)
7. a (p. 565)
8. d (p. 569)
9. g (p. 578)
10. e (p. 586)

True/False

1. F (p. 561)
2. F (p. 562)
3. F (p. 562)
4. T (p. 563)
5. F (p. 565)
6. F (p. 566-567)
7. T (p. 569)
8. T (p. 572)
9. T (p. 575)
10. T (p. 581-582)
11. F (p. 587)
12. T (p. 591)

Multiple Choice

1. a (p. 562)
2. b (p. 562-563)
3. d (p. 563-564)
4. c (p. 565)
5. a (p. 567)
6. b (p. 569)
7. a (p. 571)
8. d (p. 575)
9. b (p. 576-577)
10. a (p. 580)
11. c (p. 584)
12. d (p. 584-585)
13. b (p. 587-588)
14. a (p. 591)
15. d (p. 593)

Essay

1. Page 561
2. Pages 562-563
3. Pages 570-581
4. Pages 581-584
5. Pages 584-596

CHAPTER 16

MANAGING HUMAN RESOURCES IN AN INTERNATIONAL BUSINESS

CHAPTER DESCRIPTION

This chapter describes the complexity of managing human resources internationally and provides recommendations for managing selection, training, and compensation related to international assignments as well as issues to consider relative to repatriation.

CHAPTER OBJECTIVES

1. Explain how to improve international assignments through employee selection.
2. Answer the question, "What sort of special training do overseas candidates need?"
3. Discuss the major considerations in formulating a compensation plan for overseas employees.
4. Describe the main considerations in repatriating employees from abroad.
5. Explain how building employee commitment can be a cornerstone of an employer's HR philosophy.

CHAPTER STUDY OUTLINE

I. The Internationalization of Business
   A. The growth of international business
   B. HR and the international business challenge
      1. Deployment
      2. Knowledge and innovation dissemination
      3. Identifying and developing talent on a global basis
   C. Research results
      1. Must accommodate cultural and other differences in making selection decisions
      2. Employers face many HR-related challenges

II. How Intercountry Differences Affect HRM
   A. Cultural factors
      1. Power distance
      2. Masculinity versus femininity
   B. Economic factors
   C. Labor cost factors
   D. Industrial relations factors
      1. Germany–codetermination
      2. In other countries state interferes little in relationship between employees and union
   E. European Community (EC)

III. Improving International Assignments Through Selection
   A. Why international assignments fail
      1. According to one study 16 to 50 percent of U.S. expatriate assignments end early
      2. Direct costs of failure probably rise to several hundreds of thousands of dollars
      3. Reasons for failure differ from country to country
   B. International staffing: Sources of managers
      1. Locals–citizens of the countries where they are working
      2. Expatriates–noncitizens of countries in which they are working

3. Home-country nationals–citizens of country in which the multinational company's headquarters is based
    4. Third-country nationals–citizens of a country other than the parent or the host country
    5. Reasons exist for using each type of staff
  C. International staffing policy based on perspective of corporation
    1. Ethnocentric corporation–prevailing attitude is superiority of home country attitudes, management style, knowledge, evaluation criteria, and managers
    2. Polycentric corporation–conscious belief that only host country managers can really understand host country market so foreign subsidiary should be managed by local people
    3. Geocentric corporation–assumes management candidates must be searched for on a global basis
  D. Selecting international managers
    1. Five factors identified as predicting success in foreign assignment
      a. Job knowledge and motivation
      b. Relational skills
      c. Flexibility/adaptability
      d. Extracultural openness
      e. Family situation
    2. Five factors not equally important
    3. Personal characteristics also distinguish successful managers
    4. Adaptability screening

IV. Training and Maintaining International Employees
  A. Orienting and training employees for international assignments
    1. Level 1: Focus on impact of cultural differences and on raising trainees' awareness of such differences
    2. Level 2: Get participants to understand how attitudes (both negative and positive) are formed and how they influence behavior
    3. Level 3: Provide factual knowledge about target country
    4. Level 4: Provide skill building in areas like language and adjustment and adaptation skills
    5. Also need functional skills and unified corporate culture
  B. International compensation
    1. The balance sheet approach
    2. Incentives
    3. Beyond compensation–nonmonetary factors
  C. Performance appraisal of international managers
    1. Who does appraisal
    2. Suggestions for improving expatriate appraisal process
      a. Stipulate assignment's difficulty level.
      b. Weight evaluation more toward on-site manager's appraisal than toward home-site manager's distant perceptions of employee's performance
      c. If home-site manager does actual written appraisal, use former expatriate from overseas location to provide background advice
      d. Modify normal performance criteria used for that particular position to fit overseas position and characteristics of particular locale
      d. Attempt to give expatriate manager credit for insights into functioning of operation and specifically interdependencies of domestic and foreign operations
  D. International labor relations–differences in practices
    1. Centralization
    2. Union structure
    3. Employer organization
    4. Union recognition
    5. Union security

6. Labor-management contracts
  7. Content and scope of bargaining
  8. Grievance handling
  9. Strikes
  10. Worker participation
  11. Work council
E. Safety and fair treatment abroad
  1. Orient expatriates before they leave
  2. Tell them not to draw attention to themselves
  3. Have travelers arrive at airports near departure time and wait in areas away from main traffic flow
  4. Equip expatriate's car and home with security systems
  5. Tell employees to vary departure and arrival times and take different routes to and from work
  6. Keep employees current on crime and other problems
  7. Advise employees to remain confident at all times
F. Repatriation: Problems and solutions
  1. Write repatriation agreements
  2. Assign a sponsor
  3. Provide career counseling
  4. Keep communications open
  5. Offer financial support
  6. Develop reorientation programs
  7. Build in return trips

CHAPTER STUDY QUIZZES

Match Terms with Definitions

a. power distance
b. polycentric
c. expatriates
d. repatriation
e. geocentric
f. third-country nationals
g. ethnocentric
h. home-country nationals
i. codetermination
j. adaptability screening

_____ 1. The extent to which the less powerful members of institutions accept and expect that power will be distributed equally.

_____ 2. When employees have the legal right to a voice in setting company policies.

_____ 3. Noncitizens of the countries in which they are working.

_____ 4. Citizens of the country in which the multinational company's headquarters is based.

_____ 5. Citizens of a country other than the parent or the host country.

_____ 6. Process that aims to assess the family's probable success in handling a foreign transfer and alerts a couple to personal issues a foreign move may involve.

_____ 7. The prevailing attitude of superiority of home country attitudes, management style, knowledge, evaluation criteria, and managers.

_____ 8. Assumption that management candidates must be searched for on a global basis since the best manager for any specific position anywhere on the globe may be found in any of the countries in which the firm operates.

_____ 9. A conscious belief that only host country managers can ever really understand the culture and the behavior of the host country market so the foreign subsidiary should be managed by local people.

_____ 10. The process of moving back to the parent company and country from the foreign assignment.

True/False

1. T F According to work by Hofstede, countries that rank high on masculinity value assertiveness while countries that rank high on femininity value caring.

2. T F All of the countries in the European Community have the same laws relative to such human resource issues as minimum wages.

3. T F Inability of the spouse to adjust to the international assignment is one reason that such assignments fail in the U. S.

4. T F Home-country nationals are citizens of the countries in which they are working.

5. T F Multinational companies increasingly view a successful stint abroad as a required step in developing top management.

6. T F An ethnocentric firm would staff foreign subsidiaries with host-country nationals and its home-office headquarters with parent-country nationals.

7. T F A geocentric staffing policy would seek the best people for key jobs throughout the organization regardless of nationality.

8. T F Flexibility and adaptability are important traits to consider in selecting international managers.

9. T F Level 1 training focuses on the impact of cultural differences, and on raising trainees' awareness of such differences and their impact on business outcomes.

10. T F One trend today is to not award long-term incentive pay to overseas managers since they are not involved in all operations of the firm.

11. T F Performance appraisals for international managers should be conducted only after they return home.

12. T F Repatriation is a relatively painless process for most expatriates.

Multiple Choice

1. In addition to the required technical and business skills, what other trait(s) should be considered when selecting employees for international assignments?
   a. cultural sensitivity
   b. interpersonal skills
   c. flexibility
   d. all of the above

2. One difference between incentive plans in Japan and the U. S. is that
   a. Japan doesn't use incentive plans; the U. S. does.
   b. Japan focuses on incentives for the work group; the U. S. still tends to focus on individual worker incentives..
   c. Japan provides only yearly incentives; the U. S. provides quarterly incentives.
   d. Japan only gives incentives to managers; the U. S. gives incentives to all workers.

3. In which country is codetermination the rule?
   a. Japan
   b. U. S.
   c. Mexico
   d. Germany

4. A British executive working in a Tokyo subsidiary of a U. S. multinational bank is an example of a/an
   a. local.
   b. expatriate.
   c. home-country national.
   d. third-country national.

5. Jaime is a Mexican national working in Mexico for a U. S. company. Jaime is an example of a/an
   a. local.
   b. expatriate.
   c. home-country national.
   d. third-country national.

6. All but which of the following are reasons given for using expatriates instead of locals?
   a. inability to find local candidates with the required technical competence
   b. to maintain control relative to policies and company culture
   c. desire for homogeneity of the workforce
   d. value of stint abroad for development of managers

7. Research has found what factor to generally be the most important to consider when making international assignments?
   a. flexibility
   b. family situation
   c. job knowledge
   d. extracultural openness

8. One way to assist the potential assignee and his or her family in making the decision about accepting an international assignment is to give them a/an
   a. realistic preview about problems to expect.
   b. strong recruitment effort.
   c. extra incentive pay.
   d. couple of weeks to make the decision.

9. In preparing employees for international assignments, providing factual information about the country to which they will be assigned is an example of which level of training?
   a. Level 1
   b. Level 2
   c. Level 3
   d. Level 4

10. In compensating expatriates, companies most often try to
    a. pay whatever the employee would have made at home.
    b. pay whatever is market for the country in which the employee is working.
    c. equalize purchasing power across countries.
    d. equalize purchasing power within the country.

11. Who should conduct the performance appraisal for international managers?
    a. the on-site manager with input from the home-site manager
    b. the on-site manager only
    c. the home-site manager only
    d. the home-site manager with input from the on-site manager

12. One difference between Western Europe and the U. S. relative to collective bargaining is that this is done at the
    a. plant level in Western Europe but the industry level in the U. S.
    b. enterprise level in Western Europe but the regional level in the U. S.
    c. individual level in Western Europe but the collective level in the U. S.
    d. industry or regional level in Western Europe but the enterprise or plant level in the U. S.

13. A major concern of expatriates abroad that is less likely to be a concern of managers in the U. S. is fear of
    a. not getting big raises.
    b. kidnapping.
    c. the unknown.
    d. storms.

14. The process of moving back to the parent company and country form the foreign assignment is known as
    a. readjustment.
    b. expatriation.
    c. reorientation.
    d. repatriation.

15. Expatriates often find it difficult to return to their home country because they may lose
    a. executive trappings of the overseas job such as company car and driver.
    b. the status they had in the international assignment.
    c. opportunities for promotions.
    d. all of the above.

Essays

1. Discuss how intercountry differences affect human resource management. Provide specific examples.

2. Why do international assignments fail? Are the reasons the same across countries?

3. What factors should organizations consider when selecting employees for international assignments?

4. Explain the difficulty associated with conducting a performance appraisal for an international manager.

5. What are some of the issues associated with repatriation?

ANSWER KEY

Match Terms with Definitions

1. a   (p. 616)
2. i   (p. 617)
3. c   (p. 619)
4. h   (p. 619)
5. f   (p. 619)
6. j   (p. 622)
7. g   (p. 621)
8. e   (p. 621)
9. b   (p. 621)
10. d (p. 630)

True/False

1. T   (p. 616-617)
2. F   (p. 617-618)
3. T   (p. 618-619)
4. F   (p. 619)
5. T   (p. 619)
6. F   (p. 620)
7. T   (p. 621)
8. T   (p. 621)
9. T   (p. 624-625)
10. F (p. 626)
11. F (p. 627)
12. F (p. 630-631)

Multiple Choice

1. d   (p. 613)
2. b   (p. 616-617)
3. d   (p. 617)
4. d   (p. 619)
5. a   (p. 619)
6. c   (p. 619)
7. b   (p. 621)
8. a   (p. 622-623)
9. c   (p. 626)
10. c (p. 626)
11. a (p. 627)
12. d (p. 628)
13. b (p. 629)
14. d (p. 630)
15. d (p. 630)

Essay

1. Pages 616-618
2. Pages 618-619
3. Pages 621-624
4. Pages 627-628
5. Page 630